CHUCK'S DAY OFF

CHUCK'S DAY OFF

CHUCK HUGHES

WITH JOANNA FOX

PHOTOGRAPHY BY
DOMINIQUE LAFOND

HarperCollins*Publishers*Ltd

Published by HarperCollins Publishers Ltd

First published by HarperCollins Publishers in a hardcover edition: 2013
This trade paperback edition: 2014

Photography by Dominique Lafond
www.dominiquelafond.com

Recipe styling and testing by Johanne Depelteau, James Baran and Chuck Hughes
Project management by Scott Bailey

HarperCollins books may be purchased for educational, business, or sales
promotional use through our Special Markets Department.

HarperCollins Publishers Ltd
2 Bloor Street East, 20th Floor
Toronto, Ontario, Canada
M4W 1A8

www.harpercollins.ca

Library and Archives Canada Cataloguing in Publication
information is available upon request

ISBN 978-1-44341-636-8

Printed and bound in China
PP 9 8 7 6 5 4 3 2

CONTENTS

INTRODUCTION

When I was in elementary school, my social studies teacher used to make the class do these aptitude tests to see what career paths were best suited to our personalities. Mine would always come back saying "chef," and although I didn't think that much of it at the time, I guess whoever was designing those tests knew what they were doing.

There was always something about the kitchen that made me feel comfortable and at home. If you had given me a choice between solving a math problem or jumping off a bridge, I probably would have taken the bridge, but with cooking, I was always really at ease.

When I was a young prep cook chopping onions until my hand blistered, sweat pouring down my face from the heat of the kitchen, and my feet numb from standing for so long, I used to dream of having my own restaurant. It was what drove me forward, day after day and year after year. When Garde Manger opened in 2006, I knew it was going to change my life, but I never expected just how much. Not only did I have a place where I could communicate through my food, but people actually liked what I was doing. With a little bit of rock and roll and a lot of love, I realized that my style of cooking worked as an extension of my personality: it reflected my East Coast roots and my French-Canadian upbringing. It's always been and always will be about honest, authentic food.

When I was approached to do a television show, I was extremely nervous. Even though I had a passion for food and liked the idea of getting other people excited about cooking, I didn't know if I could pull it off or how it would come across. I'm the first one to admit that I'm a big talker, but it's hard for me to tell others how much I appreciate them. So doing a show about the act of preparing a meal, gathering at the table, sharing dishes, and getting a chance to enjoy it without the chaos of the busy restaurant just felt right.

Chuck's Day Off is a glimpse into my life and what goes into making Garde Manger work. What you see on the show is the real thing. If you come by the restaurant for dinner, you will pretty much see everything exactly as it is on TV. I use my pans and my knives, my plates and my bowls, in my real restaurant kitchen. There's no smoke and mirrors going on there. The people I cook for are actual people in my life, and the menus I make for them feature things they like to eat. There is no faking, no pretending, no acting. It isn't always easy—a TV crew and cameras in a tiny kitchen make everyone's jobs harder—and I definitely never get a day off, but it is well worth all the trouble.

There are so many ingredients to a successful restaurant. Some of it is sheer luck, but most of it involves the hard work, passion, and talent of a community of people. From the staff and the suppliers to my friends and my family, these people are what *Chuck's Day Off* is all about.

Whether you want to read this book cover to cover or just check out a recipe or two, I hope it gives you insight into why I do what I do. You might recognize some of the characters I introduced on the show and my all-time favourite dishes that I made for them, but there are also stories you've never heard before and lots of new recipes to try. More than just an accompaniment to the TV series, this book is about the important people in my life and how they've defined who I am today.

I cook because I love it, and honestly there's nothing else in the world I'd rather do. Cooking makes me happy because I see how much pleasure I can give others. Whether I'm doing it at work or on my day off, cooking allows me to connect with people on a fundamental level while expressing who I am with each dish.

If there is one thing I've learned from this whole restaurant and TV show experience, it's that you never know where life is going to take you or who will be along for the ride. Food brings people together, and that alone can go a really long way.

SUPPLIERS

When I used to dream as a young cook about having my own restaurant, I figured all I needed was a solid crew of people to make and serve food exactly the way I wanted, and that was it. What I didn't realize then was how my relationships and, more importantly, my friendships with my suppliers would be key to having a successful restaurant.

Many of my suppliers I knew way before I opened Garde Manger. Some of them I met when I was a kid, some as a teenager, and the rest when I started out cooking professionally. Never would I have imagined that they would still be with me today.

If there's one thing that the people who are close to me or have worked with me know, I'm loyal to a fault. But to earn that loyalty takes time. In this extremely competitive industry, a lot of people are fickle, but I've been incredibly lucky with all my suppliers. These people are experts in their fields, and I know that they have both my restaurant and my best interests at heart. In turn, these are the people I keep going back to with absolute confidence in their word and their products or services.

No matter where you live, chances are there are people like this in your food community. I know it may be convenient to go to the supermarket and do all your shopping in one place, but I have to tell you, dealing with quality suppliers and having access to the excellent products they offer makes all the difference in your cooking. Not only that, but they're there to help you, to answer your questions, make suggestions, and introduce you to new ingredients. Instead of getting your steak from a supermarket aisle, get it from the person who butchered the cow. You can ask your fishmonger what's in season and what came in fresh that day. Whether you're buying mushrooms, olive oil, wine, or cheese, knowing your suppliers is a good way to learn more about the products you like and where they come from.

Among my valued suppliers, there's my Greek landlords who also supply me with oils, olives, and honey; the spice guys at Les Douceurs du Marché; the whole team at my favourite seafood store, La Mer; my French butchers at Boucherie de Tours; my truffle guy, Paolo; my cheese guy, Gilles; Mohamed, who takes care of all our coffee needs; Theo the wine expert; and Norm at Metro Linen.

I strongly believe that the success of Garde Manger has a lot to do with these people, who are more than just suppliers—they're friends I trust. Looking back on seven years trying to make my place work, I can't imagine getting anywhere in this business without them.

THE
LANDLORDS

Fried Feta Salad
Skordalia and Taramasalata
Panzanella with Grilled Asparagus and Garlic Shrimp
Pan-Fried Skate with Tzatziki

When we first walked into the location that would one day become Garde Manger, the place was disgusting. It was owned by a blind man who was about eighty-two years old, and I don't think he'd been in there for a while. It had once been an Italian restaurant called Pavarotti, and before that it was rumoured to have been one of Montreal's hottest gay clubs in the 1970s.

I say it was disgusting because it really was. It was all boarded up, dark, dank, dusty, and the basement scared the shit out of me. But for my partners and me, who were just starting out, it was a dream come true. We didn't want to spend a ton of money on a pristine place full of pink marble. (Besides, we didn't *have* any money.) We wanted our restaurant to be rustic, authentic, and totally DIY. We felt that for a few guys who weren't afraid to put a lot of hard work into it, the place had amazing potential. I think it took us all of ten minutes to decide that we wanted to open our first restaurant here.

The basement was jam-packed with treasures. There were vintage bottles, taxidermic geese, butcher scales, weird old signs, and tons of other knick-knacks. Almost everything you see on our walls today was found in that basement. The massive chandelier that hangs from the ceiling was salvaged from an old Montreal movie theatre, the Palace. My partners and I put everything we had into Garde Manger, and all our blood and sweat and tears (and yes, there were tears) definitely paid off.

A month after we signed our lease, the blind man sold the building to George Tsoudis, who turned out to be the best landlord a restaurant could ask for. George and his brother Costa are Greek guys who together own a bunch of real estate around the city as well as a depanneur in Mile End called Variety Delphi, a pimped-out

convenience store and post office where they also sell outstanding Greek products imported from their family.

George and Costa supply the restaurant with olive oil, kalamata olives, and Cretan honey, and we really see eye to eye on quality. They're always bringing us new discoveries to try, and whenever we need to find some elusive Greek product, they always help. They once got us the biggest wheel of Greek cheese I have ever seen—it almost broke a shelf in my fridge! At Christmas, they give everyone at the restaurant a bottle of olive oil or honey. I'm so happy that these are the kind of people I do business with.

George may be our landlord, but more importantly, he's my friend (and he's really funny). We text a lot, and he's never afraid to call me out on things or make fun of me. If he hears about me judging a cupcake competition, I get a text. If he sees me having an intimate moment with my beloved dog Filou, I get a text. If my hair gets too long, I get a text. If he sees me doing something embarrassing on TV, I get a text.

George is just someone I can relate to, and I know he's always going to have my back. His Greek roots inspired this menu. So to George, Costa, and all their family—*opa!*

FRIED FETA SALAD

PREP 20 MIN × COOK 5 MIN × SERVES 4 TO 6

Fried feta is a recent discovery of mine, and I don't know what took me so long to try it. After all, I like to fry everything! It's a great way to change up a Greek salad.

DRESSING
- 1/4 cup (60 mL) sour cream
- 2 tablespoons (30 mL) olive oil
- 2 tablespoons (30 mL) red wine vinegar
- 1 tablespoon (15 mL) chopped fresh oregano
- 1 small garlic clove, minced
- Salt and freshly cracked black pepper

SALAD
- 6 to 8 medium heirloom tomatoes, halved
- 1 shallot, thinly sliced
- 1 English cucumber, peeled, seeded, and cubed
- 1/4 cup (60 mL) pitted kalamata olives, chopped
- 1 tablespoon (15 mL) chopped fresh dill
- 1 tablespoon (15 mL) chopped fresh chives
- 1 tablespoon (15 mL) chopped fresh mint
- 1 tablespoon (15 mL) olive oil
- 1 teaspoon (5 mL) red wine vinegar
- Maldon sea salt and freshly cracked black pepper

FRIED FETA
- Canola oil for deep-frying
- 1 cup (250 mL) all-purpose flour
- Salt and freshly cracked black pepper
- 2 eggs
- 2 cups (500 mL) feta cheese, cut in chunks

FOR THE DRESSING:
In a small bowl, whisk together the sour cream, olive oil, vinegar, oregano, and garlic. Season with salt and pepper.

FOR THE SALAD:
In a large bowl, combine the tomatoes, shallot, cucumber, olives, dill, chives, and mint. Add the olive oil and vinegar; toss gently. Season with Maldon salt and pepper.

FOR THE FRIED FETA:
In a deep-fryer or deep, heavy saucepan, heat 3 inches (8 cm) of canola oil to 350°F (180°C).

In a shallow dish, stir together the flour, salt, and pepper. Beat the eggs in a second shallow dish. Working in batches if necessary, dredge the chunks of feta in the flour, then dip in eggs. Dredge in flour again, coating thoroughly. Deep-fry until golden brown, about 2 minutes.

Drain on paper towels. Season with salt and pepper.

To serve, drizzle a spoonful of the dressing over each plate. Top with salad and garnish with fried feta.

SKORDALIA AND TARAMASALATA

Here are two authentic Greek dips. Skordalia is made by blending garlic with bread to form a thick, spreadable paste, and taramasalata is fish roe mixed with creamy mashed potatoes.

SKORDALIA

PREP 15 MIN × SERVES 4

- 2 garlic cloves, peeled
- 1 head of roasted garlic (page 150)
- 1 cup (250 mL) toasted walnuts
- 2 slices country bread, soaked in milk or stock
- 1/2 cup (125 mL) extra-virgin olive oil
- Juice of 1 lemon
- Coarse salt and freshly cracked black pepper

In a food processor, purée the fresh garlic, roasted garlic, and walnuts. Squeeze the bread dry. Add the bread to the garlic mixture along with the olive oil and lemon juice; season with salt and pepper. Process until smooth.

Transfer to a bowl and refrigerate until ready to serve. If the mixture stiffens up, thin it with a little olive oil or water.

Serve as an antipasto with taramasalata, grilled baby octopus, grilled vegetables, and warm pitas. It's also a great accompaniment to grilled lamb, fish, or chicken or cold leftover roast chicken.

COOK'S NOTE:
Traditional skordalia calls for 8 to 10 cloves of fresh garlic, but I tamed this one by using mostly mellower roasted garlic.

TARAMASALATA

PREP 20 MIN × COOK 15 MIN × SERVES 4

- 1 large potato, peeled and cut in cubes
- 2 garlic cloves
- 8 oz (225 g) good-quality tarama (carp or codfish roe)
- 1 small shallot, minced
- Zest and juice of 1 lemon
- 1 teaspoon (5 mL) Dijon mustard
- About 1 cup (250 mL) olive oil
- Salt and freshly cracked black pepper

Place the potato and garlic in a small saucepan and cover with salted water. Bring to a boil, reduce heat, and simmer until the potato is cooked through. Drain and set aside to cool a bit. Mash the potato and garlic until very smooth.

In a blender, combine half of the tarama, the shallot, lemon zest and juice, and mustard; blend until smooth. With the motor running, add the olive oil in a steady stream until the mixture is creamy. Pour over the mashed potatoes, add the remaining tarama, and stir well. Season with salt and pepper.

Serve with bread or crackers.

COOK'S NOTE:
You can make this using milk-soaked bread instead of mashed potatoes. With bread, it is saltier and more textured. With potato, it is sweeter and smoother. Some cooks combine both starches. Replace the potato with about 2 slices of bread.

PANZANELLA WITH GRILLED ASPARAGUS AND GARLIC SHRIMP

PREP 30 MIN PLUS 2 HOURS FOR SOAKING × COOK 15 MIN × SERVES 4 TO 6

The key to this bread-based salad is a trick my landlord showed me: you rub the bread with garlic and tomato *before* it goes in this traditionally Italian dish. The addition of dandelion greens adds a bitter Greek kick.

- 4 slices day-old sourdough bread, cubed
- About 1/2 cup (125 mL) olive oil
- Salt and freshly cracked black pepper
- 1 garlic clove, smashed
- 3 or 4 large tomatoes, halved crosswise
- A bunch of dandelion greens, tough stems discarded, leaves torn
- Leaves from a bunch of basil
- 12 cherry tomatoes, halved
- 1 red bell pepper, charred, peeled, seeded, and diced
- 1/2 red onion, thinly sliced
- 8 caper berries
- 1/2 lb (225 g) asparagus, cut in 1-inch (2.5 cm) pieces, blanched
- 12 medium shrimp, peeled (tail shells left intact) and deveined
- Juice from 1/2 lemon
- 8 oz (225 g) burrata, mozzarella di bufala, or feta cheese

Preheat oven to 400°F (200°C).

Place the bread on a baking sheet lined with parchment paper. Drizzle with some olive oil and season with salt and pepper. Bake for 10 minutes or until the bread is golden brown.

Rub the croutons with the garlic, then mince the garlic; set aside. Put the croutons in a large bowl. Squeeze the tomato halves over the croutons to allow their juices to soak in. Coarsely chop the tomatoes; add to the croutons, drizzle with some olive oil, and toss. Let sit at room temperature for 2 hours for the croutons to soak up all the tomato juice and olive oil.

Meanwhile, in a medium bowl, combine the dandelion greens, basil, cherry tomatoes, roasted pepper, red onion, and caper berries; toss. Set aside in the refrigerator.

When ready to serve, heat a cast-iron grill pan over medium-high heat. Drizzle a little olive oil over the asparagus, season with salt and pepper, and place in the pan; grill for 2 minutes. Add asparagus to the croutons; toss. Heat 1 tablespoon (15 mL) of the olive oil in the same pan. Add the shrimp; sauté for 1 minute on each side. Stir in the reserved garlic. Season with salt and pepper. Remove from heat.

To serve, add the dandelion salad to the crouton mixture; sprinkle with lemon juice and toss well.

Cut the burrata cheese and divide it among salad plates. Season with salt and pepper. Pile the panzanella salad and the garlic shrimp on top.

PAN-FRIED SKATE
WITH TZATZIKI

PREP 10 MIN PLUS 60+ MIN FOR DRAINING × COOK 5 MIN × SERVES 4

Skate is definitely not the handsomest fish in the sea, but its flaky white meat is light, delicious, and perfect with home-made tzatziki. Be sure to get your skate from a reputable and environ-mentally responsible supplier.

TZATZIKI

- 1 English cucumber, half-peeled, seeded, and diced
- 1/2 Vidalia onion, diced
- Salt and freshly cracked black pepper
- 2 cups (500 mL) plain Greek yogurt
- 3 garlic cloves, minced
- 1/2 cup (125 mL) chopped fresh dill
- 1/2 cup (125 mL) chopped fresh chives
- 1 tablespoon (15 mL) olive oil
- Juice of 1 lemon

SKATE

- 1 cup (250 mL) all-purpose flour
- 4 eggs, beaten
- 2 cups (500 mL) dry bread crumbs
- 4 skinless skate fillets
- 2 tablespoons (30 mL) canola oil
- Salt and freshly cracked black pepper
- Lemon wedges for garnish

FOR THE TZATZIKI:

In a sieve set over a bowl, toss the cucumber and onion with 1 teaspoon (5 mL) salt. Let drain for at least 1 hour at room temperature, or cover and refrigerate for up to 8 hours. Wrap the cucumber and onions in a kitchen towel and squeeze to remove as much liquid as possible. Pat dry with paper towels. Transfer to a bowl and add the yogurt.

Mash the garlic with 1/2 teaspoon (2 mL) salt to make a paste. Add the garlic paste to the cucumber mixture; add the dill, chives, olive oil, and lemon juice. Stir well. Season with salt and pepper. Refrigerate until ready to use.

FOR THE SKATE:

Have ready in 3 shallow dishes the flour, eggs, and bread crumbs. Coat the skate with flour, then egg, then bread crumbs.

In a large skillet, heat the oil over medium-high heat. Fry the skate for 2 minutes on each side. Season with salt and pepper.

Serve with the tzatziki and lemon wedges.

THE
SPICE GUYS

Grilled Mackerel with Green Olive Pesto and Cauliflower Purée
Chicken with Chorizo, Crispy Rock Shrimp, and Gravy on Soft Polenta
Mussels with Bacon and Rapini
Balsamic Swirl Ice Cream

My all-time favourite shop at Montreal's Atwater Market has got to be Les Douceurs du Marché. I grew up in the small country town of St-Sauveur just north of the city, so when I first moved to Montreal as a kid, it was sensory overload for my eight-year-old brain. My school principal, Ms. Saunders, lived in our apartment building with her son, and on weekends she would take both of us to the Atwater Market. As a treat we'd go to this cool little shop, Les Douceurs du Marché, where she would buy us each a Jamaican patty. I'd never tasted anything like it—so easy to eat and so good! Where had they been all my life? A little later on, when I went to the market with my mom, I would beg her to let me stop for one. It became our Atwater Market tradition.

I always loved going into Les Douceurs, but at first it used to make me really nervous. There was so much stuff to knock over or break—shelves packed with bottles of hot sauces, olive oils, and balsamic vinegars from all over the world, glass cases filled with chocolate—it was daunting for a kid like me who wanted to get his hands on everything. My mom would always warn me not to touch anything, but c'mon! Everything looked so cool! Today, Les Douceurs du Marché is my one-stop shop for specialty products, from olive oil to gourmet pasta, teas, hot sauces, grains, and especially spices. I still get excited whenever I enter this store.

Some ingredients in my kitchen have been essential Les Douceurs finds, like Jamaican jerk spice. It all started when one of my friends and co-workers, Chris, had jerk crab at a Jamaican friend's place. Everyone was raving about how good it was. So Chris and I decided to make our own jerk spice and replicate the

dish. First we went to Les Douceurs and bought some jerk in a jar. It was pretty darn good, but we were determined to make it ourselves. We spent a while experimenting with ingredients and techniques until finally we realized that using the jar of paste from the spice guys and giving it a little twist was the best approach. Crab's delicate, sweet taste mingling with that spicy jerk kick is an amazing combination! I don't think my customers would ever forgive me if I took the dish off the menu, and although ours is not a traditional Jamaican jerk because it's done in a pan instead of on a grill, I have to say, it's pretty awesome. I can't get enough of our jerk spice—I put it in sandwiches, in mayonnaise, on meat. I have to keep myself in check, otherwise I would use it in everything!

Every month, I still have to go to Les Douceurs du Marché and check out what they've got. I always discover something new. Once, while I was working on a potato chip recipe, I stopped by the store. They showed me this smoked salt that had just come in and suggested I try it on my chips. It honestly took those deep-fried potato slivers to a new level of greatness, and from that day on, we always have smoked salt on hand.

We have a smoker and could make our own smoked salt if we wanted to, but we already have a long list of things to do each day. As much as it's fun to make things from scratch, if you find a good-quality commercial product, I don't see anything wrong with taking a little shortcut once in a while. Stuff like smoked salt, jerk spice, and some of the other products we get from Les Douceurs are great alternatives that I've come to appreciate using in my everyday cooking, at the restaurant and at home.

The whole team at Douceurs—Erica, Amedee, Benoit—are great people, knowledgeable, friendly, and willing to find anything you might need. And there's something about their store that just brings out the kid in me.

GRILLED MACKEREL WITH GREEN OLIVE PESTO AND CAULIFLOWER PURÉE

PREP 15 MIN × COOK 11 MIN × SERVES 4

Not only is mackerel a sustainable fish but it's also rich in omega-3 oils. Cauliflower purée is a delicious alternative to potatoes, and green olive pesto adds saltiness and a burst of colour.

GREEN OLIVE PESTO

- 2 cups (500 mL) fresh basil leaves
- 2 cups (500 mL) fresh parsley leaves
- 1 cup (250 mL) pitted green olives
- 1/2 cup (125 mL) grated Parmigiano-Reggiano cheese
- 1/2 cup (125 mL) olive oil
- 1/4 cup (60 mL) toasted almonds
- Salt and freshly cracked black pepper

CAULIFLOWER PURÉE

- 1 head cauliflower, cut in small pieces
- 2 tablespoons (30 mL) butter
- Salt and freshly cracked black pepper

GRILLED MACKEREL

- 2 tablespoons (30 mL) olive oil
- 12 mackerel fillets
- Salt and freshly cracked black pepper
- 1/4 cup (60 mL) toasted almonds, coarsely crushed, for garnish
- Good olive oil for garnish

FOR THE OLIVE PESTO:

In a blender, combine the basil, parsley, olives, Parmesan, olive oil, and almonds; blend until smooth. Season with salt and pepper. Transfer to a bowl, cover, and refrigerate if not using soon.

FOR THE CAULIFLOWER PURÉE:

Cook the cauliflower in boiling salted water until tender, about 10 minutes. Drain. Transfer to a food processor, add the butter, and process until smooth. Season with salt and pepper. Keep warm.

FOR THE GRILLED MACKEREL:

Heat the oil in a cast-iron grill pan over medium-high heat. Cook the mackerel, skin side down, for 1 minute. Remove from heat. Season with salt and pepper.

To serve, spoon some cauliflower purée over the bottom of each plate. Top with 3 fillets of mackerel. Garnish each fillet with a spoonful of the olive pesto. Sprinkle with almonds. Drizzle with some good olive oil.

COOK'S NOTE:

You can replace mackerel with sardines, smelts, or herring.

CHICKEN WITH CHORIZO, CRISPY ROCK SHRIMP, AND GRAVY ON SOFT POLENTA

PREP 15 MIN × COOK 60 MIN × SERVES 4

This grab bag of flavours is influenced by Spain, Italy, and the U.S.A. Although you could travel to all these countries, it's probably a lot cheaper just to make this finger-licking dish, which packs a delicious smoky, sweet punch.

CHICKEN WITH CHORIZO
- Leaves from 6 sprigs of rosemary, chopped
- Salt and freshly cracked black pepper
- 8 boneless, skin-on chicken thighs
- About 1/4 cup (60 mL) olive oil
- 2 fresh chorizo sausages, sliced
- 1 lb (450 g) cipollini onions, peeled
- 4 garlic cloves, minced
- 1/2 cup (125 mL) chicken stock

GRAVY
- 1 tablespoon (15 mL) all-purpose flour
- 1 cup (250 mL) chicken stock

- 1 tablespoon (15 mL) cold butter
- Salt and freshly cracked black pepper

SOFT POLENTA
- 2 cups (500 mL) chicken stock
- 2 cups (500 mL) milk
- 3 sprigs of cilantro
- 2 garlic cloves, smashed
- 1 cup (250 mL) cornmeal
- 1 cup (250 mL) grated Asiago or Parmigiano-Reggiano cheese
- Salt and freshly cracked black pepper

CRISPY ROCK SHRIMP
- Canola oil for deep-frying
- 2 cups (500 mL) cornstarch
- 1/2 cup (125 mL) all-purpose flour
- Salt and freshly cracked black pepper
- 4 eggs
- 1 lb (450 g) rock shrimp, peeled

FOR THE CHICKEN WITH CHORIZO:
In a small bowl, combine half of the rosemary with 1 teaspoon (5 mL) salt and pepper to taste. Using your fingertips, gently loosen the skin from the chicken, being careful not to tear it. Rub half of the rosemary mixture under the skin. Coat the outside of each chicken piece with a little olive oil and rub with the remaining rosemary mixture.

Preheat oven to 350°F (180°C).

In a large ovenproof skillet over high heat, heat half of the olive oil. Add the chicken, skin side down, and cook until browned, about 5 minutes. Transfer to a plate. Add the chorizo to the pan, along with some of the remaining oil if necessary, and cook until browned on both sides, about 2 minutes. Using a slotted spoon, remove the chorizo and add to the chicken.

Reduce heat to medium. Add the onions, along with some of the remaining oil if necessary, and cook, stirring occasionally, until softened and browned, about 20 minutes. Add the garlic and cook for 30 seconds. Stir in the stock and remaining rosemary. Return the chicken and chorizo to the pan, cover, and transfer to the oven. Bake, basting occasionally, until the chicken is no longer pink inside, about 30 minutes.

Transfer chicken and chorizo to a plate and cover loosely with foil to keep warm.

FOR THE GRAVY:

Sprinkle the flour over the pan juices and cook, stirring, over medium heat until the flour is golden brown. Stir in the stock and continue to cook, stirring, until the gravy thickens. Pass through a sieve set over a saucepan. Whisk in the butter. Season with salt and pepper.

FOR THE SOFT POLENTA:

In a large, heavy saucepan, combine the stock, milk, cilantro, and garlic. Bring to a boil, reduce heat to medium, and simmer for 2 minutes to flavour the liquid. Discard the cilantro and garlic. Reduce heat to low. Whisking constantly, add the cornmeal in a steady stream; cook, stirring often, until the polenta is soft, 10 to 15 minutes. Remove from heat. Fold in the cheese and season with salt and pepper. Cover and keep warm.

FOR THE CRISPY ROCK SHRIMP:

In a deep-fryer or deep, heavy saucepan, heat 3 inches (8 cm) of canola oil to 350°F (180°C).

In a bowl, stir together the cornstarch, flour, and salt and pepper. In another bowl, beat the eggs. Working in batches if necessary, coat the shrimp in the beaten eggs, then in the cornstarch mixture. Deep-fry until golden-brown, about

2 minutes. Drain on paper towels. Season with salt and pepper.

To serve, gently reheat the gravy. Place a large spoonful of soft polenta on each plate. Top with chicken and chorizo, ladle the gravy over top, and garnish with the shrimp.

MUSSELS WITH BACON AND RAPINI

PREP 20 MIN × COOK 20 MIN × SERVES 4

Mussels may seem daunting, but they're really easy to make—and inexpensive. The bacon adds the perfect amount of rich, smoky flavour, and the rapini is bright, peppery, and bitter. It really is a perfect combination.

- 8 slices thick-cut bacon, diced
- 4 thick slices crusty bread, cubed
- 1 teaspoon (5 mL) steak spice
- 2 tablespoons (30 mL) olive oil
- 1 onion, sliced
- About 12 red cherry tomatoes
- 1 cup (250 mL) white wine
- 2 lb (900 g) mussels, scrubbed and debearded
- 1 cup (250 mL) water
- 1/2 bunch rapini, blanched, drained, and chopped
- 2 tablespoons (30 mL)
- butter
- 1/4 cup (60 mL) chopped fresh dill
- 1/4 cup (60 mL) finely chopped fresh chives
- Salt and freshly cracked black pepper

In a large skillet, cook the bacon over medium heat until crispy, about 5 minutes. Remove from the pan with a slotted spoon and drain on paper towels. Add the bread cubes to the pan and toss so they soak up the bacon fat. Sprinkle with the steak spice and cook, stirring occasionally, until the croutons are golden and crisp. Remove from the pan and set aside.

In the same pan, heat the olive oil. Add the onion and sauté for 2 minutes. Add the cherry tomatoes and continue cooking for 5 minutes. Add the wine; cover and cook for 2 minutes. Add the mussels and water, cover, and cook until the mussels begin to open, 5 to 7 minutes. Stir in the rapini and butter; cook until rapini is heated through.

Remove from heat and discard any unopened mussels. Stir in the bacon, dill, and chives. Season with salt and pepper. Serve with the croutons on top.

BALSAMIC SWIRL ICE CREAM

PREP 30 MIN × COOK 12 MIN PLUS 4 HOURS FOR FREEZING × MAKES 6 CUPS (1.5 L)

You don't need good-quality balsamic vinegar for this recipe, so save the pricey stuff for salads. Adding sweet, tangy balsamic to this vanilla ice cream always leaves people wanting more!

- 4 cups (1 L) whipping cream
- 1 vanilla bean
- 6 large egg yolks
- 1 cup (250 mL) sugar
- 2 cups (500 mL) balsamic vinegar
- 1 cup (250 mL) fruity extra-virgin olive oil
- Fresh berries for garnish

Place half of the cream in a small saucepan. Scrape the seeds from the vanilla bean into the cream, then add the pod. Warm over medium heat for about 2 minutes.

Meanwhile, in a medium bowl, whisk together the egg yolks and half of the sugar until the mixture is pale, about 3 minutes. Remove the vanilla pod from the cream. Stirring constantly, add the warm cream to the egg mixture. Return the mixture to the saucepan and cook, stirring constantly, over low heat until the custard thickens enough to coat the back of a spoon, about 3 minutes. Let cool, then refrigerate.

Meanwhile, in a saucepan, reduce the balsamic vinegar by half, about 10 minutes. Let cool.

When your custard is cold, in a large bowl, whip the remaining cream and sugar together until soft peaks form. Fold in the custard mixture. Fold in the olive oil. Drizzle 3/4 cup (175 mL) of the balsamic reduction over the cream mixture; using a fork, make swirl patterns. Pour the mixture into a large container and drizzle with the remaining balsamic reduction.

Cover with plastic wrap and freeze until firm, at least 4 hours.

To serve, scoop into nice bowls and serve with fresh berries.

THE FISH GUYS

ROASTED HALIBUT WITH SMOKED TOMATO VINAIGRETTE
HOME-SMOKED SALMON AND NORDIC SHRIMP SALAD
ROASTED GARLIC WHELKS
SEAFOOD CHILI WITH WALLEYE

I've been obsessed with the ocean my whole life. It was probably from my mom that I inherited the idea of life at sea being a mysterious, romantic adventure. I can sit in any port in the world and simply watch the boats come in and set out, wondering about the people on them. If I didn't love my life here in Montreal, I think I'd be just as happy living by the water, wearing gumboots and serving oysters out of a shack. Stay tuned . . .

With a good half of my family from New Brunswick, the Maritimes are a part of me. When I first moved to Montreal from the country, I lived at Habitat 67, then an ultra-modern building, designed by Moshe Safdie for Montreal's Expo 67. It has an incredible view of the city and overlooks one of the oldest inland seaports in North America. When my mom and I would walk around the area (it wasn't as developed or touristy as it is now), we'd see men going into bars along the waterfront. My mom would always tell me, "Those are the sailors, Charles." (I think my mom's "sailors" were drunks and homeless people, but what can I say, the lady's a romantic.)

My mom would take me to food fairs around the city where local producers and suppliers would showcase what they had to offer. One Montreal seafood store, La Mer, always had a booth, and I would go over and talk to them, try some oysters, and ask lots of questions. In particular I remember Richard, who captured my attention with his vast knowledge of everything fish-related. He was such a cool and interesting guy, my mom would literally have to drag me away.

Years later, when I started working in restaurants, the guys from La Mer were usually the ones who supplied the seafood. By then Richard had moved to the Gaspé region, but another guy, Costa, was always around. Costa and I became good friends, and today La Mer is my go-to place for fish and seafood.

My style of cooking has a huge seafood focus—I'm a freak for the stuff—so getting the best that's out there is essential. I try to focus as much as I can on what's local and seasonal, because in Montreal we have access to everything Quebec has to offer as well as all the great stuff from the East Coast of Canada. Oysters, lobsters, shrimp, crabs, scallops, salmon, trout, mackerel, sea urchins—it's all incredible, fresh, and Canadian.

Sustainability is an important priority for us, and questions about what is right to eat and what is wrong arise daily. It's important to understand where our fish and seafood comes from, how it gets to our plates, and how that ultimately affects our lakes, rivers, and oceans. The more informed I am, the better decisions I can make about what I want to eat and serve. I believe that whenever possible, we should try to eat sustainably caught fish and seafood. Knowing the people who sell me my fish and asking them questions makes me more conscious of my choices.

La Mer has always been good to me, from when I was an annoying little kid asking questions at those food fairs all the way to today, when I badger them endlessly for the freshest and best out there. We're partners helping each other succeed. La Mer never lets me down, and in return, they're my guys.

ROASTED HALIBUT WITH SMOKED TOMATO VINAIGRETTE

PREP 10 MIN × COOK 30 MIN × SERVES 4

Build your own smoker by using a wok and a bamboo steamer on your stovetop and give these tomatoes an awesome woodsy, outdoor flavour. The flaky white meat of halibut is the perfect match for every mouthful of this refreshing (and healthy!) dish.

SMOKED TOMATO VINAIGRETTE

- 2 handfuls of hickory wood chips, soaked in water for 1 hour
- 1 cup (250 mL) water
- 8 medium ripe red tomatoes (any variety)
- Leaves from 1 large sprig of tarragon
- 2 shallots, sliced in rings
- Coarse salt and freshly cracked black pepper
- 2 tablespoons (30 mL) red wine vinegar
- 1 cup (250 mL) olive oil

ROASTED HALIBUT

- 4 skin-on halibut fillets (4 oz/115 g each)
- Coarse salt and freshly cracked black pepper
- 1 tablespoon (15 mL) canola oil
- A handful of baby greens or micro-greens
- 1 shallot, thinly sliced

FOR THE SMOKED TOMATO VINAIGRETTE:

Prepare a wok smoker: Line a large bamboo steamer with parchment paper. Lay two sheets of foil in the bottom of a wok. Place drained wood chips on top. Turn heat to high. Add the water. Quarter and seed the tomatoes. Pop into the bamboo steamer; add tarragon and shallots. Season with salt and pepper. Set the steamer inside the smoking wok. Cover and smoke for 20 minutes.

Place tomatoes in a blender. With the motor running, add red wine vinegar, then drizzle in the olive oil until you get a smooth consistency. Adjust seasoning and set aside.

FOR THE ROASTED HALIBUT:

Preheat oven to 375°F (190°C).

Season the halibut with salt and pepper. In a large ovenproof skillet, heat the oil over high heat. Add the halibut, skin side down, and cook until golden brown on the bottom, 3 to 4 minutes. Flip the fillets and cook for another 3 minutes. Place the pan in the oven and roast the fish until it is snowy white and firm to the touch, about 5 minutes. (Be careful not to overcook it, or it will be dry.)

To serve, toss the baby greens with the shallot. Ladle the smoked tomato vinaigrette into deep plates. Top with a piece of halibut, and place a few baby greens on top.

HOME-SMOKED SALMON & NORDIC SHRIMP SALAD

PREP 90 MIN PLUS 12 HOURS FOR MARINATING × COOK 30 MIN × SERVES 8

Curing and smoking salmon is something that everyone should try. Adding a Nordic shrimp salad and fried Jerusalem artichokes puts the finishing touches on the perfect Maritime meal.

HOME-SMOKED SALMON

- 2 cups (500 mL) coarse salt
- 2 cups (500 mL) brown sugar
- 1 skin-on fresh salmon fillet (2 lb/900 g)
- Freshly cracked black pepper
- 2 handfuls of hickory wood chips, soaked in water for 1 hour
- 1 cup (250 mL) water
- 1 cup (250 mL) ice cubes

SOUR CREAM AND DILL DRESSING

- 1/4 cup (60 mL) whipping cream
- Juice of 1 lemon
- 1/4 cup (60 mL) sour cream
- 2 tablespoons (30 mL) finely chopped fresh chives

- 2 tablespoons (30 mL) chopped fresh dill
- A pinch of cayenne pepper
- Salt and freshly cracked black pepper

NORDIC SHRIMP SALAD

- 2 English cucumbers, thinly sliced
- 1 teaspoon (5 mL) coarse salt
- About 3 cups (750 mL) mâche
- 1 cup (250 mL) cooked Matane or Nordic shrimp
- 1/2 cup (125 mL) fresh peas or chickpeas (optional)
- Maldon sea salt and freshly cracked black pepper

FRIED JERUSALEM ARTICHOKES

- Canola oil for deep-frying
- 8 Jerusalem artichokes, washed and thinly sliced lengthwise
- Coarse salt and freshly cracked black pepper

FOR THE HOME-SMOKED SALMON:
In a bowl, stir together the salt and brown sugar. Rub the salt mixture all over the salmon. Place the salmon on a plate, cover with plastic wrap, and refrigerate for 12 hours.

Rinse the salt mixture off the salmon and pat dry with paper towels. Lay the salmon on a platter lined with a lint-free kitchen towel and refrigerate for 1 hour to dry out.

Prepare a wok smoker: Line a large bamboo steamer with parchment paper. Lay two sheets of foil in the bottom of a wok. Place drained wood chips on top. Turn heat to high. Add the water and ice cubes. Place the salmon in the bamboo steamer. Season with pepper. Set the steamer inside the smoking wok. Cover and smoke, keeping the temperature under 150°F (65°C), for 30 minutes or until the salmon is firm to the touch and the edges are a little browner, crustier, and caramelized.

FOR THE SOUR CREAM AND DILL DRESSING:
In a bowl, whisk together the cream and lemon juice. Stir in the sour cream, chives, dill, and cayenne. Season with salt and pepper. Set aside.

FOR THE NORDIC SHRIMP SALAD:
In a sieve set over a bowl, toss the cucumber with the coarse salt. Let drain for at least 1 hour at room temperature, or cover and refrigerate for up to 8 hours. Rinse cucumbers and pat dry with paper towels. Set aside.

In a medium bowl, stir together the mâche, shrimp, and peas (if using). Season with salt and pepper. Set aside.

FOR THE FRIED JERUSALEM ARTICHOKES:
In a deep-fryer or deep, heavy sauce-pan, heat 2 inches (5 cm) of canola oil to 350°F (180°C). Deep-fry artichoke slices until golden brown and crispy. Drain on paper towels. Season with salt and pepper.

To serve, slice the smoked salmon about 1/4 inch (5 mm) thick.

Arrange cucumber slices in a thin layer on a serving plate. Top with smoked salmon.

Mix the shrimp salad with some of the dressing. Top the salmon with the salad. Season with Maldon salt and pepper. Garnish with fried Jerusalem artichokes.

COOK'S NOTE:
Letting the salmon dry out for 1 hour will allow the smoke to adhere to the flesh more easily.

ROASTED GARLIC WHELKS

PREP 1 HOUR 20 MIN PLUS 30 MIN FOR SOAKING × COOK 25 MIN × SERVES 4

When I was a kid my mom used to bring me back jars of pickled whelks from the East Coast of Canada, and I couldn't get enough of them. Also called sea snails, whelks are similar to escargots but even tastier.

WHELKS

- 4 lb (2 kg) small to medium live whelks
- 1 cup (250 mL) coarse salt
- 4 cups (1 L) water
- 1 tablespoon (15 mL) sea salt
- 1 tablespoon (15 mL) hot pepper sauce
- Juice of 1 lemon
- 2 bay leaves

ROASTED GARLIC BUTTER

- 1/2 cup (125 mL) butter, softened
- 2 fresh red chilies, seeded and finely chopped
- 1 head of roasted garlic (page 150)
- 1 garlic clove, minced
- 2 tablespoons (30 mL) chopped fresh parsley
- 1 tablespoon (15 mL) minced fresh chives
- Zest of 1 lemon
- About 4 large croutons, crushed
- Salt and freshly cracked black pepper

FOR SERVING

- Chopped fresh parsley
- Crusty country bread

FOR THE WHELKS:

Wash the whelks in water, then drain them. In a large bowl, dissolve the coarse salt in the water; add the whelks. Let sit for about 30 minutes. Drain the whelks and rinse under cool running water for about 20 minutes, giving them a good stir every so often.

Place the whelks in a large saucepan, cover them with water, and add the sea salt, hot pepper sauce, lemon juice, and bay leaves. Bring to a boil, then simmer gently for 20 minutes. Remove from heat and let cool for about 1 hour. When the whelks are cool enough to handle, drain them and remove them from the shells with a small skewer or lobster pick. Remove and discard the small, disc-like piece of shell attached to the body and the dark grey sac. Rinse the shells and dry on paper towels.

Preheat broiler.

FOR THE ROASTED GARLIC BUTTER:

In a bowl, stir together the butter, chilies, roasted garlic, minced garlic, parsley, chives, lemon zest, and crushed croutons. Season with salt and pepper.

To finish, place the whelks back in their shells and place in 1 large or 4 individual ovenproof serving skillets. Top each whelk with some of the roasted garlic mixture. Broil for 2 minutes or until warm and the butter is melted. Garnish with parsley and serve immediately with crusty bread.

SEAFOOD CHILI WITH WALLEYE

PREP 30 MIN × COOK 6 HOURS 20 MIN × SERVES 4 TO 6

A homemade chicken stock really sets this chili apart. Whenever I make stock, I make more than I need for one recipe. Freeze the leftovers and you'll have great stock ready in a pinch.

CHICKEN STOCK
(MAKES ABOUT 8 CUPS/2 L)

- 2 tablespoons (30 mL) canola oil
- Bones of 1 whole chicken
- 2 large carrots, peeled and coarsely chopped
- 2 celery ribs, chopped
- 2 medium onions, chopped
- 1 leek (white and pale green parts only), chopped
- 1 head of garlic, top sliced off to expose the cloves
- A bunch of parsley
- 4 sprigs of thyme
- 2 sprigs of rosemary
- 1 tablespoon (15 mL) black peppercorns
- About 16 cups (4 L) water
- Coarse salt and freshly cracked black pepper

WALLEYE

- 4 skin-on walleye fillets (4 oz/115 g each)
- Coarse salt and freshly cracked black pepper
- 2 tablespoons (30 mL) olive oil

SEAFOOD CHILI

- 1 tablespoon (15 mL) olive oil
- 2 Yukon Gold potatoes, peeled and diced

- 1 onion, diced
- 1 carrot, diced
- 1 celery rib, diced
- 1 red bell pepper, diced
- 1 garlic clove, minced
- 1 fresh red chili, minced
- 1 teaspoon (5 mL) ground cumin
- 3 cups (750 mL) chicken stock
- Coarse sea salt and freshly cracked black pepper
- 1/4 cup (60 mL) whipping cream
- 2 lb (900 g) clams, scrubbed (see note)
- 1/2 lb (225 g) rock shrimp or Nordic shrimp
- 8 large scallops, cut in 4 lengthwise
- 1 cup (250 mL) fresh crabmeat (from about 4 snow crab legs)

FOR THE STOCK:

In a stockpot, heat the oil over medium-high heat. Add the chicken bones, stirring to coat with oil. Cook, stirring occasionally, for 5 minutes or until the bones are browned. Add the carrots, celery, onions, leek, and garlic. Cook, stirring frequently, until the vegetables are slightly brown. Stir in the parsley, thyme, rosemary, and peppercorns. Add the water. Bring to a simmer, skimming any scum from the surface. Reduce heat to medium and simmer, uncovered and without stirring, for 4 to 6 hours, skimming off any scum. Strain and skim off the fat. Season with salt and pepper.

FOR THE WALLEYE:

Season the walleye with salt and pepper. In a large skillet, heat the oil over high heat. Sear the walleye, skin side down, for 2 minutes or until the skin is crispy and golden brown. Turn and continue cooking for 2 minutes. Remove from heat.

FOR THE SEAFOOD CHILI:

In a large skillet, heat the oil over medium-high heat. Add the potatoes, onion, carrot, and celery. Sauté until the onions are translucent, about 5 minutes. Stir in the red pepper, garlic, chili, and cumin. Add the stock. Season with salt and pepper. Add the cream and clams, cover, and cook for 5 minutes or until the clams start to open. Add the walleye and shrimp; cook for 2 minutes. Add the scallops and crab; continue cooking for 1 minute. Remove from heat and season with salt and pepper. Discard any unopened clams. Serve in large shallow bowls with crusty bread.

COOK'S NOTE:

BC savoury clams are sustainably farmed and have a delicate and sweet flavour. Little Necks (or little-necks) are the smallest commonly available East Coast hard-shell clam. They are delicious raw, steamed, or roasted.

THE
BUTCHERS

DIRTY LEG OF LAMB

SPINACH GRATIN

DUCK-FAT FRIES WITH HOMEMADE MAYONNAISE

MOLTEN WHITE CHOCOLATE CARAMEL CAKES

When I was young, I loved going to the Atwater Market, and when I was a teenager, I actually worked there, in a sausage shop. They made all their own sausages, terrines, and pâtés, but I was hired mainly to serve the customers. Even though I worked only at that one shop, everyone at the market was like a big family, and I got to know all the different shop owners and employees. The experience taught me a bunch of things, but most important, I learned to have a lot of respect for anyone who worked with meat. It requires skill, knowledge, and a pretty steady hand—you really have to pay attention to what you're doing! I witnessed that both at the sausage shop and watching the guys working at Boucherie de Tours, right next door. I never forgot how good those butchers were, and from the day I opened Garde Manger, I've been buying from them.

You have to trust your butcher. I've been working with Boucherie de Tours for a long time, and I can say with certainty that I'm getting the best possible product. The owner, Monsieur Fortier, who opened the store in 1983, is a pleasure to work with. I speak with him every time I call to make an order, and he really goes above and beyond when I'm in a pinch. The butcher, Monsieur Baudry, is a true Frenchman who uses traditional French techniques and always wears a red beret. Not only are his knife skills incredible but he also wrote a cookbook in French, which (translated) is called *Everything You Ever Wanted to Know About Meat But Were Afraid to Ask*. He's a huge advocate for the local farming industry and supplies some of the best Quebec lamb in the city. Finally there is Monsieur André, who does the deliveries. A real gent, he loves to talk about what's on the menu and what we're making this week. He never hesitates to let me know about new arrivals and different cuts I might be interested in.

Although our menu can be very seafood focused, our meat dishes are just as important. One of our most popular meat items is our braised beef short ribs, but we also do the quintessential flank steak, and any time I put a beef tartare on the menu, people go wild for it. I have to say, though, that for me, pork is where it's at. I even have a tattoo that says "bacon"!

One of our most important ingredients, however, is one that most of our customers probably never notice: our veal stock. We use it as a base for sauces, braises, risottos, and even some of our vegetable dishes. It's like liquid gold in our kitchen. The quality of our veal stock is essential to the quality of our dishes, so we can't mess around with it. For a good stock we need good bones. In fact, we go through so much veal stock, we don't have enough leftover bones to make it. So every Monday, Boucherie de Tours delivers us veal bones, and we begin making a giant batch of stock. We start by slowly roasting the bones to heighten all the delicious flavours. Then they go into a pot with their juices, bits of meat, vegetables, herbs, and water, lots of water. Then we simmer it, wait until it's ready to strain, and reduce it even further.

Although we do use other butchers for specific products, we're definitely not alone in recognizing Boucherie de Tours's unmatched quality and service. Like many other well-known Montreal restaurants, we call these people first for anything to do with meat. Oh, and in case you're wondering, they eventually bought the little sausage shop next door.

DIRTY LEG OF LAMB

PREP 15 MIN × COOK 1½ HOURS × SERVES 8

This is the ultimate in festive food and ideal if you're cooking for a big group. The black olives give the sauce a deep, dark colour. This lamb looks and tastes spectacular.

- 1 bone-in lamb leg (5 lb/2.25 kg)
- 2 tablespoons (30 mL) olive oil
- Kosher salt and freshly cracked black pepper
- 2 tablespoons (30 mL) canola oil
- 3 tablespoons (45 mL) Dijon mustard
- 1/2 cup (125 mL) pistachios, toasted and chopped
- 2 tablespoons (30 mL) honey
- 1 onion, sliced
- 1 leek (white and pale green parts only), chopped
- 1 head of garlic, top sliced off to expose the cloves
- 3 sprigs of rosemary
- 3 sprigs of thyme
- 4 sprigs of mint
- 1/2 cup (125 mL) pitted kalamata olives, crushed
- 4 cups (1 L) veal stock

Preheat oven to 325°F (160°C).

Rub the lamb all over with the olive oil. Season with salt and pepper.

Heat the canola oil in a large roasting pan over high heat. Add the lamb and sear on all sides, about 5 minutes. Remove from heat. Brush the lamb with the mustard and coat with the pistachios, pressing gently if needed to help the nuts adhere. Drizzle with the honey.

Add the onion, leek, garlic, rosemary, thyme, mint, olives, and veal stock to the pan. Cover with a lid or foil. Transfer to the oven and cook for 1½ hours for medium-rare.

Slice the lamb and serve with a generous serving of the sauce straight from the pan. Serve with Spinach Gratin (page 44) and Cheese and Caramelized Shallot Popovers (page 119).

SPINACH GRATIN

PREP 15 MIN × COOK 25 MIN × SERVES 6

What's the easiest way to make fussy eaters finish their spinach? Add some cheese!

- 3 tablespoons (45 mL) butter
- 2 lb (900 g) baby spinach
- 1 onion, chopped
- 1 garlic clove, minced
- 2 tablespoons (30 mL) all-purpose flour
- 1 cup (250 mL) whipping cream
- 1 cup (250 mL) milk
- 1 tablespoon (15 mL) Dijon mustard
- 2 cups (500 mL) shredded Emmental cheese
- Kosher salt and freshly cracked black pepper

Preheat oven to 400°F (200°C). Butter an 8-cup (2 L) gratin dish.

In a large skillet over medium-high heat, melt 1 tablespoon (15 mL) of the butter. Add the spinach and cook, stirring occasionally, until just wilted, 3 to 4 minutes. Transfer to a bowl and let cool. Using your hands, press out excess water.

In the same skillet over medium heat, melt the remaining 2 tablespoons (30 mL) butter. Add the onion and cook, stirring, until translucent, about 5 minutes. Stir in the garlic. Add the flour and cook, stirring constantly, until just golden, about 1 minute. Slowly whisk in the cream and milk. Add the mustard. Cook, stirring, until the sauce is thickened, about 3 minutes. Add half of the Emmental cheese; stir until melted. Pour the sauce over the spinach and fold to combine. Season with salt and pepper. Transfer to the prepared gratin dish and top evenly with the remaining cheese. Bake until golden brown on top, about 10 minutes.

DUCK-FAT FRIES WITH HOMEMADE MAYONNAISE

PREP 30 MIN PLUS 1 HOUR FOR SOAKING × COOK 12 MIN × SERVES 4

Once you taste fries cooked in duck fat, you'll never want them any other way. You can get duck fat at most good butchers.

HOMEMADE MAYONNAISE
- 1 large egg
- 2 tablespoons (30 mL) red wine vinegar
- 1 tablespoon (15 mL) Dijon mustard
- 2 cups (500 mL) canola oil
- 1 teaspoon (5 mL) salt
- Freshly cracked black pepper

DUCK-FAT FRIES
- 6 Yukon Gold potatoes
- 6 cups (1.5 L) duck fat
- Maldon sea salt and freshly cracked black pepper

FOR THE HOMEMADE MAYONNAISE:
In a blender or food processor, blend the egg with the vinegar and mustard. With the motor running, slowly add the canola oil until the mixture is emulsified and very creamy. Add a little water to thin the consistency if necessary. Season with salt and pepper. Refrigerate if not using immediately.

FOR THE DUCK-FAT FRIES:
Cut the potatoes into strips 1/2 inch (1 cm) thick. Soak in cold salted water for 1 hour.

In a large, deep saucepan, heat the duck fat to 275°F (140°C). Drain the potatoes and pat dry with paper towels. Fry in batches until tender but not colouring, 5 to 7 minutes. Drain on paper towels and let cool. Heat the fat to 375°F (190°C), then fry the potatoes in batches until golden and crisp, 3 to 5 minutes. Drain on paper towels and season with Maldon salt and pepper. Serve with the mayo.

MOLTEN WHITE CHOCOLATE CARAMEL CAKES

PREP 15 MIN × COOK 12 MIN × SERVES 6

Sometimes using chocolate in desserts can get a bit predictable, so give 'em something different with this white chocolate and caramel treat! Sprinkle a dusting of Maldon salt on top to finish and you've created a dessert to die for.

- 2 cups (500 mL) chopped white chocolate
- 1/4 cup (60 mL) unsalted butter
- 2 cups (500 mL) dulce de leche
- 4 large eggs, at room temperature
- 1/4 cup (60 mL) sugar
- 1 cup (250 mL) all-purpose flour
- Maldon sea salt

Preheat oven to 425°F (220°C).

Butter six 4-oz (125 mL) ramekins; place ramekins on a baking sheet.

In a saucepan over low heat, melt the white chocolate with the butter, stirring slowly until smooth, about 10 minutes. Stir in the dulce de leche. Set aside.

In a large bowl with an electric mixer, beat the eggs with the sugar until the mixture is pale and has doubled in volume. Fold in the chocolate mixture. Fold in the flour.

Divide the batter among the ramekins. Bake for 12 minutes or until the cakes are golden brown but the middle is still soft. Serve sprinkled with Maldon salt.

THE TRUFFLE GUY

Truffle Bread Pudding with Poached Eggs and Truffle
Chicken Suprêmes with Truffles and Sage
Roasted Jerusalem Artichokes
Chocolate Truffles with Maldon Salt

I'm always amazed at how some ingredients intimidate people. Usually the more expensive items, like foie gras and caviar, are the culprits. Truffles fall into this category too. People try them at restaurants but would never use them in their home kitchens. To be honest, I was a late passenger on the truffle train myself because, the way I see it, unless you're a mushroom-loving millionaire, they're not for everyday use. But I've grown comfortable enough cooking with them to incorporate these pricey fungi into several dishes.

Another reason people shy away from truffles is that they associate them with truffle oil. Let's get one thing straight: truffles and truffle oil are like night and day! Given my own bad experiences with a heavy-handed dose of potent truffle oil, I was expecting a punch in the face when I first had a truffle. The reality is that truffles are very aromatic and have a delicate, subtle taste. When you get the real deal, you'll know them by their unbelievable fragrance. It varies from region to region, but the strong scent is woodsy, slightly nutty, and earthy.

Highly coveted and in demand all over the world, white truffles from Italy's Piedmont region are, per pound, one of the most expensive foods out there. Black truffles (also coined black diamonds) from the Périgord district of France are considered the best money can buy. Because truffles grow underground, usually at the foot of oak trees, truffle hunters used to train pigs to identify the scent and zero in on where they were growing. Unfortunately, these truffle-loving pigs were caught once too often gobbling up the buried treasure, so now it's more common to use man's best friend.

When I was starting out as a cook and truffles came into the restaurant, they were practically kept under lock and key. I wouldn't
even get to smell them! And because I never got to work with them,
I lost interest in them. I didn't understand that when chefs spend
about $200 on a single ingredient, they are very cautious about
using it—and letting a kitchen novice like me waste it.

So I was pretty reluctant to use truffles at Garde Manger, but
my friend and truffle dealer Paolo is so knowledgeable about them,
and has so much experience with them, he put me right at ease.
With quality and freshness paramount to his business, Paolo gets
his truffles flown in straight from Italy. When Paolo shows up with
his cooler full of truffles, it's always a fun delivery that fascinates
the whole restaurant. There's no denying that truffles are a luxuri-
ous product, and the more Paolo taught me about them, the more
interesting they became to me. Once I decided to use them, it was a
match made in truffle heaven.

I've since learned that one of the best and easiest ways to use a
truffle is as a garnish, very thinly shaved over pizza, pasta, risotto,
and the ultimate, a poached egg. Treat it almost as if you were sprinkling herbs or Parmesan cheese on top of your dish in a nice thin,
even layer so that it blends in for a delicate but decadent flavour.

I understand why people don't normally use truffles at home, but
at a restaurant, it's easy to give them a try. The truth of the matter
is, though, at the restaurant they're probably about three times the
price, so if you're interested in truffles and want to give them a shot,
I suggest you buy one and make the most of it in your own kitchen.
Here are a few recipes to inspire you.

TRUFFLE BREAD PUDDING WITH POACHED EGGS

PREP 15 MIN PLUS 3 HOURS FOR SOAKING × COOK 50 MIN × SERVES 8

Egg and truffle is a match made in heaven, and this dish is even better with the addition of Gruyère cheese.

TRUFFLE BREAD PUDDING
- 1 brioche loaf (1 lb/450 g)
- 6 large eggs
- 3 cups (750 mL) milk
- Salt and freshly cracked black pepper
- 1 small Italian black truffle, shaved, some shavings reserved for garnish (optional)
- Leaves from 2 sprigs of thyme, chopped
- 2 tablespoons (30 mL) olive oil
- 2 cups (500 mL) dried morels, rehydrated
- 2 cups (500 mL) stemmed chanterelles
- 1 shallot, minced
- 4 cups (1 L) shredded Gruyère cheese

POACHED EGGS
- 6 eggs
- 1 tablespoon (15 mL) white vinegar

SALAD
- 4 cups (1 L) mixed micro-greens
- 1 tablespoon (15 mL) olive oil
- 1 teaspoon (5 mL) good-quality sherry vinegar
- Salt and freshly cracked black pepper

FOR THE TRUFFLE BREAD PUDDING:

Cut the brioche into 1-inch (2.5 cm) cubes. In a large bowl, whisk together the eggs and milk. Season with salt and pepper. Add the brioche, truffle, and half the thyme; stir to coat the brioche with the egg mixture. Cover with plastic wrap and refrigerate for at least 3 hours or overnight.

Preheat oven to 350°F (180°C).

Heat the oil in a large skillet over medium-high heat. Sauté the morels, chanterelles, and shallot until the mushrooms are brown. Remove from heat and stir in the remaining thyme. Season with salt and pepper. Let cool for about 5 minutes. Add the mushrooms and half of the Gruyère cheese to the bread pudding mixture; fold to combine.

Pour the mixture into a large baking dish. Top evenly with the remaining cheese. Bake for 45 minutes or until puffed and golden brown.

FOR THE POACHED EGGS:

Fill a saucepan with 3 inches (8 cm) of cold water, add a pinch of salt, and bring to a boil. As the water reaches the boiling point, reduce the heat until the water just simmers. Add the vinegar.

Break an egg into a small plate or bowl. With a spoon, swirl the simmering water to create a whirlpool in the centre. Gently slip the egg into the centre, holding the plate as near to the water as possible. Repeat with the remaining eggs. You can help shape the eggs using a spoon or spatula. Poach the eggs for 3 to 3½ minutes, or until preferred doneness.

Remove each egg with a slotted spoon and drain it for a few seconds on a kitchen towel. Trim any dangling bits with a knife or scissors if you wish.

FOR THE SALAD:

Toss together the micro-greens, olive oil, sherry vinegar, and salt and pepper.

To serve, spoon the truffle bread pudding onto warm plates. Top with a poached egg and garnish with a little salad and some shaved truffle if using.

CHICKEN SUPRÊMES WITH TRUFFLES AND SAGE

PREP 20 MIN × COOK 45 MIN × SERVES 4

A suprême is a more sophisticated cut of chicken breast that still has its wing bone attached. Using an old cooking trick, I stuff the truffles and sage under the skin to add extra flavour.

SAUCE

- 2 cups (500 mL) chicken stock
- 1 tablespoon (15 mL) Dijon mustard
- Juice of 1/2 lemon
- 1 cup (250 mL) butter, melted
- Bits and pieces from the sliced truffle (see below)
- Salt and freshly cracked black pepper

CHICKEN

- 4 chicken suprêmes
- 1 small fresh black truffle, thinly sliced
- Leaves from 6 sprigs of sage
- Salt and freshly cracked black pepper
- 1 tablespoon (15 mL) olive oil

FOR THE SAUCE:

Simmer the chicken stock to reduce by half, about 30 minutes. Stir in the mustard and lemon juice. Slowly whisk in the butter, whisking constantly until emulsified. Remove from heat. Stir in the truffle. Season with salt and pepper. Keep warm. Whisk before serving.

FOR THE CHICKEN:

Preheat oven to 350°F (180°C).

Separate the skin from the breast and wing by carefully inserting a finger and gently pushing between the skin and meat. Insert the truffle slices under the loosened skin over the breast and wing meat. Cover with sage leaves, then gently press the skin back into place. Season with salt and pepper.

In a large skillet, heat the oil over high heat. Add the chicken, skin side down, and cook until the skin is golden. Transfer the pan to the oven and bake for 10 minutes or until the chicken is just cooked through.

Serve with the sauce and Roasted Jerusalem Artichokes (page 57).

ROASTED JERUSALEM ARTICHOKES

PREP 5 MIN × COOK 45 MIN × SERVES 4

Also known as sunchokes, Jerusalem artichokes are actually a species of sunflower and are considered a root vegetable. Don't drive yourself nuts trying to peel them for this recipe; just pop them in the oven and enjoy their sweet, creamy goodness.

- 1 lb (450 g) Jerusalem artichokes, washed, halved lengthwise
- 3 tablespoons (45 mL) olive oil
- Salt and freshly cracked black pepper

Preheat oven to 350°F (180°C).

In a bowl, toss the artichokes with the olive oil. Season with salt and pepper. Spread on a baking sheet, cut side down. Bake for 45 minutes or until caramelized and tender.

CHOCOLATE TRUFFLES with MALDON SALT

PREP 25 MIN × COOK 5 MIN PLUS 3 HOURS FOR CHILLING × MAKES 40 TRUFFLES

If you're not into the earthier kind of truffles, these ones are sure to please. They're easy to make—and even easier to eat!

- 2½ cups (625 mL) chopped dark chocolate (1 lb/450 g)
- 1 cup (250 mL) whipping cream
- 1 vanilla bean
- 1 tablespoon (15 mL) Maldon sea salt

Place 1½ cups (375 mL) of the chocolate in a medium bowl. In a saucepan, heat the cream with the vanilla bean over medium-low heat until simmering, about 5 minutes. Discard the bean. Pour the hot cream over the chocolate and stir until melted and smooth. Cover and refrigerate the ganache until firm, about 2 hours.

Using two teaspoons, scoop a portion of the ganache into your hand, then roll it between your palms to form a ball. Place the ball on a baking sheet. Repeat with the remaining ganache, refrigerating the balls if your kitchen is warm.

Melt the remaining 1 cup (250 mL) chocolate in a saucepan or the microwave. Use two spoons to roll each ball in the melted chocolate. Transfer to a baking sheet lined with parchment paper. Sprinkle with salt. Chill until firm, about 1 hour. (*Can be made 1 week ahead. Store in an airtight container, layers separated with wax paper, and keep chilled.*) Let stand at room temperature for 1 hour before serving.

COOK'S NOTE:

To make maple sugar truffles, add crushed toasted pecans to the ganache. Sprinkle the coated truffles with maple sugar and Maldon salt.

THE CHEESE GUY

CRISPY FRIED CHEESE SQUARES
HOMEMADE RICOTTA CHEESE AND TOMATO SALAD ON ROASTED GARLIC CROUTONS
MARGHERITA PIZZA
LEMON MADELEINES

People compare Quebec with France for many reasons. The most obvious are that we speak French and were once a French colony. Then there's food. We are both extremely passionate about our food and we take some products, like our cheeses, very seriously.

From the cheese makers to the cheese shops, there's no shortage of standout varieties here, and we don't mind spending a little extra to get what we want. In Quebec we can use unpasteurized, or raw, milk as a base for many of our local offerings, an approach also inherited from France. Using these traditional methods results in what some connoisseurs believe to be a superior product.

When it comes to the business side of food, I think a universal etiquette requires one to always be professional and respectful toward those who are serious about what they do. I learned this lesson from my cheese supplier back when I was working my first head chef job at a restaurant called Time Supper Club.

When I went shopping at the Atwater Market on my days off, one of my favourite stops was La Fromagerie Atwater, a premier cheese shop in Montreal. Not only did they have an awesome selection, but they had a staff of very cute girls, and I liked to flirt while buying my cheese. I would usually go during the week when it was relatively quiet, but one time I happened to be there on a Saturday when the store was packed. I went up to the girls and started doing my usual shtick with no regard for the fact that I was probably a huge distraction to them. All of a sudden the owner, Gilles, grabbed my arm, looked me straight in the eye, and said, "Do you want cheese or not?"

After reflecting on what had happened, I realized that Gilles had taught me what it means to be a business owner who takes pride in his store and *his* products. I was in *his* place, distracting *his* staff, and—just as if someone were distracting *my* cooks in *my* kitchen—I was totally out of line. I think back to that day whenever I need to remind a customer that as much as Garde Manger is a fun place to be, my staff still have jobs to do.

I have the utmost respect for Gilles. A true bon vivant and epicurean, he's regarded as a Montreal cheese pioneer and guru. Whenever there's anything I want to know, he's the guy I ask. He has owned La Fromagerie Atwater since 1983 and sells cheese from all over the world, and especially from Quebec. An ambassador for Quebec's thriving industry, he's a wealth of information and seems to know about every producer and variety in the province. The best part is that all his staff are equally engaged about cheese, and they'll let you taste anything.

Cheese makes the world a better place, I say. So far in my life, I have yet to taste a cheese that I didn't like. In any shape, state, or stinkiness, I'll eat them all. When I was a kid, I used to get two cheese snacks in my lunch every day at school. One was called La Vache Qui Rit, or Laughing Cow. It came in circular packs made up of individually wrapped wedges, and to this day I can't resist them. The other cheese, a real kid's treat, was the Babybel, a disc of cheese coated in red wax. Once you ate the cheese, you had a perfect wax shell to fit nicely on your nose—or on the kid's next to you. Fun *and* delicious!

In the restaurant, we use all sorts of cheeses in many different ways. We fry it, melt it, crumble it, slice it, shave it, make it into sauces, and, obviously, put it on our poutine. Speaking of which, I'm going to say this once, and I'm not going to say it again: If poutine is not made with squeaky white Quebec cheese curds, it's not the real thing.

CRISPY FRIED CHEESE SQUARES

PREP 15 MIN PLUS 3 HOURS FOR CHILLING × COOK 10 MIN × SERVES 6

These crispy, gooey bites of goodness are some of the best finger-food I know. They can be prepared in advance, frozen, and then tossed in the fryer when you're ready to serve.

- 1/2 cup (125 mL) butter
- 1 garlic clove, smashed
- 1½ cups (375 mL) all-purpose flour
- 2 cups (500 mL) milk
- 1½ cups (375 mL) shredded Emmental cheese (6 oz/170 g)
- 1½ cups (375 mL) shredded Gruyère cheese (6 oz/170 g)
- 1 cup (250 mL) grated Parmigiano-Reggiano cheese (6 oz/170 g)
- 1 teaspoon (5 mL) cayenne pepper
- Salt and freshly cracked black pepper
- Canola oil for deep-frying
- 4 eggs, beaten
- 1 cup (250 mL) dry bread crumbs

Line a 13- × 9-inch (3.5 L) cake pan with plastic wrap.

Melt the butter in a saucepan over medium-low heat. Add the garlic, then stir in 1 cup (250 mL) of the flour. Cook, stirring constantly, for 2 minutes. Whisk in the milk; cook, stirring constantly, until the sauce thickens. Bring to a boil, add the cheeses, and continue stirring until melted and smooth. Season with cayenne, salt, and pepper. Discard the smashed garlic.

Pour cheese mixture into the prepared cake pan. Cover and refrigerate until firm, at least 3 hours. Invert the cheese mixture onto a work surface; remove the plastic wrap. Cut into 12 squares. (*Can be rewrapped in plastic wrap and frozen for up to 1 month. Thaw before using.*)

In a deep-fryer or deep, heavy saucepan, heat 3 inches (8 cm) of canola oil to 350°F (180°C). Place the remaining 1/2 cup (125 mL) flour, the eggs, and the bread crumbs in 3 separate shallow dishes. Season each with salt and pepper.

Working in batches, dredge each cheese square in the flour, then dip in the eggs, letting excess drip off, and finally coat with the bread crumbs. Fry until golden brown, about 2 minutes. Drain on paper towels.

....

COOK'S NOTE:
You can substitute any other semi-soft or firm cheese you like.

....

HOMEMADE RICOTTA CHEESE AND TOMATO SALAD ON ROASTED GARLIC CROUTONS

PREP 30 MIN × COOK 45 MIN × SERVES 6

Making your own ricotta may sound daunting, but this simple cheese takes only about 30 minutes to prepare and will literally give you a taste of what cheese makers do.

HOMEMADE RICOTTA CHEESE

- 8 cups (2 L) whole milk
- 2 cups (500 mL) buttermilk
- 1 cup (250 mL) whipping cream
- Salt

TOMATO SALAD

- 6 to 8 assorted ripe heirloom tomatoes, sliced
- 2 cups (500 mL) baby arugula
- Greek basil leaves, to taste
- 2 tablespoons (30 mL) good-quality extra-virgin olive oil
- Maldon sea salt and freshly cracked black pepper
- 1 tablespoon (15 mL) Balconville vinegar or good-quality balsamic vinegar

ROASTED GARLIC CROUTONS

- 2 tablespoons (30 mL) olive oil
- 6 thick slices country bread
- 1 head of roasted garlic (page 148)

FOR THE RICOTTA:

In a large pot, heat the milk, buttermilk, and cream over medium heat until a candy thermometer reads about 185°F (85°C). Reduce the heat to low to maintain this temperature. (The mixture should not boil or the curd will break.) Let rest on the heat, without stirring, until a white curd forms at the surface, about 30 minutes. The yellowish whey will separate from the curd.

Line a colander with 3-ply cheesecloth; place in the sink. Pour the curd into the colander and let drain for 30 to 45 minutes. For drier ricotta cheese, let it drain longer in the refrigerator. Transfer to a bowl. Season with salt to taste. (*If not using immediately, cover with plastic wrap and refrigerate for up to 3 days.*)

FOR THE TOMATO SALAD:

In a large bowl, toss together the tomatoes, arugula, basil, and olive oil. Season with Maldon salt and pepper. Set aside.

FOR THE ROASTED GARLIC CROUTONS:

In a skillet, heat the oil over medium heat. Add the bread and grill until toasted on both sides. Spread roasted garlic on the croutons.

To serve, spread some ricotta on the roasted garlic croutons. Top with the tomato salad. Drizzle with Balconville vinegar. Season with Maldon salt and freshly cracked black pepper.

....

COOK'S NOTE:

Balconville vinegar is an apple vincotto that is made with late-harvest Empire apples by Quebec's Société-Orignal. Syrupy and sweetly acidic, it is comparable to the finest balsamic vinegars of Italy.

....

MARGHERITA PIZZA

PREP 30 MIN PLUS 4 HOURS FOR RESTING × COOK 40 MIN × SERVES 6

Pizza is pretty much the perfect food, so I think that every night is a good night to have a pizza party. Use a Piave that has aged for at least 1 year; look for Piave vecchio in specialty cheese stores.

PIZZA DOUGH

- 1 cup (250 mL) warm water
- 1/2 tablespoon (7.5 mL) active dry yeast
- 1/2 tablespoon (7.5 mL) sugar
- 1/2 tablespoon (7.5 mL) olive oil
- 2¼ cups (560 mL) all-purpose flour
- 1 teaspoon (5 mL) salt

MARINARA SAUCE

- 3 tablespoons (45 mL) olive oil
- 1 small onion, chopped
- 2 garlic cloves, minced
- 1 can (19 oz/540 mL) chopped tomatoes
- Salt and freshly cracked black pepper
- Leaves from a bunch of oregano, chopped

MARGHERITA PIZZA

- 1 cup (250 mL) marinara sauce
- 6 oz (170 g) mozzarella di bufala, cut in chunks
- 2 cups (500 mL) grated aged Piave or Parmigiano-Reggiano cheese
- Fresh basil leaves for garnish

FOR THE PIZZA DOUGH:

In a large bowl, stir together the water, yeast, sugar, and olive oil. Let stand for about 5 minutes, until the mixture starts to foam. Add the flour and salt; stir until the dough comes together. Transfer to a lightly floured surface and knead until smooth, about 5 minutes. Place the dough in a lightly oiled large bowl and turn it to coat with oil. Cover with plastic wrap and refrigerate for at least 4 hours or overnight.

FOR THE MARINARA SAUCE:

Heat the oil in a medium saucepan over medium heat. Add the onions and sauté until translucent. Add the garlic and continue to cook for a few minutes until fragrant. Add the tomatoes; cook, stirring occasionally, for 30 minutes. Season with salt and pepper. Remove from heat. Using an immersion blender, blend until smooth. Stir in the fresh oregano. You'll likely have a bit more than the cup you need for the pizza, so either go heavy on the sauce or keep it for a bit of dipping action later.

FOR THE MARGHERITA PIZZA:

Preheat oven to 500°F (260°C) with the rack in the middle. If you have a pizza stone feel free to use it, but you don't need one.

Shape the pizza dough into a ball. On a floured surface, roll out the dough to a diameter of about 12 inches (30 cm). Drizzle with olive oil. Set the dough on an upside-down baking sheet that has been lightly oiled with olive oil. Spread 1 cup (250 mL) of the marinara sauce over the dough, leaving a border of about 1 inch (2.5 cm). Garnish with the mozzarella chunks and the grated Piave.

TO BAKE THE PIZZA:

Slide the baking sheet onto the middle rack. Bake for 10 minutes or until the crust is golden brown. Garnish the pizza with basil leaves and a drizzle of olive oil.

COOK'S NOTE:

Feel free of course to experiment with your pizza toppings. I really like goat cheese, fennel, and sausage with caramelized onions.

LEMON MADELEINES

PREP 20 MIN PLUS 2 HOURS FOR CHILLING × COOK 15 MIN × MAKES 36 MADELEINES

Madeleines are the quintessential French sweet. If you want the traditional look, you'll need a special baking pan with shell-shaped cups. Otherwise, this recipe works just as well using mini-muffin pans.

MADELEINES

- 4 large eggs
- 1 cup (250 mL) sugar
- Zest and juice of 1 lemon
- 1 teaspoon (5 mL) vanilla extract
- 1½ cups (375 mL) all-purpose flour
- 1 teaspoon (5 mL) baking powder
- 1 cup (250 mL) butter, melted and cooled to room temperature

LEMON GLAZE

- 1/2 cup (125 mL) icing sugar
- Zest and juice of 1 lemon

FOR THE MADELEINES:
Generously butter and flour madeleine moulds.

In a medium bowl with an electric mixer, beat the eggs with the sugar until the mixture is thick and pale, about 5 minutes. Beat in the lemon zest and juice, then the vanilla. In another bowl, whisk together the flour and baking powder. In portions, fold the flour into the egg mixture, then fold in the butter. Divide the batter among the moulds, filling each cup three-quarters full. Cover with plastic wrap and refrigerate for at least 2 hours.

Preheat oven to 425°F (220°C).

Bake madeleines for 15 minutes or until golden brown and a toothpick comes out clean. Turn the madeleines out onto racks and turn scalloped side up.

FOR THE LEMON GLAZE:
In a small bowl, combine the icing sugar, lemon zest, and juice; stir until smooth. One at a time, drag the tops of the warm madeleines through the glaze. Set aside and let cool completely.

....

COOK'S NOTE:
Refrigerating the madeleines and then baking them at a high temperature will help them rise.

....

THE
COFFEE GUY

PORK BELLY WITH COFFEE GLAZE AND SCALLOPS
BLACK COD RATATOUILLE WITH HERB SALAD
AFFOGATO
DARK CHOCOLATE, ESPRESSO, AND PISTACHIO BISCOTTI

The coffee machine at Garde Manger is our version of the water cooler, where everyone goes to hang out and chat when they get to work. First in are the prep cooks, then the cooks, then the dishwashers, then the floor staff—they all make themselves a coffee, and once that's finished, they know it's time to get started.

For me, it's my quiet morning ritual. I get to the restaurant early, and before I do anything, I go straight for the coffee machine. It gives me that five minutes to relax, clear my head, and just sit there sipping away before the day really begins. You know how every coffee commercial starts? It's basically like that, a Folgers jingle in my head as I drink my macchiato.

Whoa, hold on a second. Did I just say macchiato?

The truth of it is, I never actually drank coffee before we opened Garde Manger. I don't know how I managed all those years of late nights without being fuelled by big cups of piping hot, black filtered coffee because these days, I'm totally hooked. I need my macchiato in the morning and I need a couple shots of espresso throughout the afternoon.

Coffee culture has evolved a lot in the past few years, and today people are interested in where their beans come from and how their coffee is made. And of course everyone has an opinion about where to get the best coffee. If I want an exceptional experience, I go all the way across town to a spot called Caffè San Simeon, in Little Italy. If you're lucky enough to get Antonio, the older Italian man who works there, you're in for a treat. It takes him five minutes to brew a perfect cappuccino, and he makes it with so much ness for a while, and I first met him when I was working at Globe. Years later, when we were fixing up Garde Manger before it opened, he saw my partners and me standing outside the restaurant. He walked over, took one look at their ridiculously oversized cups of coffee, and asked why they were drinking such ghetto brew. I explained we didn't have a proper machine yet—we were in the early days of construction and barely had a working toilet. Four hours later Mohamed was back with a machine, a grinder, coffee beans, cups, and even sugar. He didn't charge us, he didn't ask us for anything, he just said, "Here you go, guys. Good luck." And that's how Mohamed became our coffee supplier.

I could easily be that gas-station dollar-a-cup rocket-fuel kind of guy, but I've really come to appreciate quality coffee. That being said, in a pinch I will drink just about anything—as long as it's not decaf!

PORK BELLY WITH COFFEE GLAZE *and* SCALLOPS

PREP 30 MIN PLUS 12 HOURS FOR CURING × COOK 3½ HOURS × SERVES 6

If you're like me and you love bacon, you're going to freak out when you try pork belly. In this recipe, the classic pairing of pork and shellfish is given a bittersweet twist with an espresso glaze.

CURING THE PORK BELLY

- 1/4 cup (60 mL) coarse salt
- 1/4 cup (60 mL) brown sugar
- 1 tablespoon (15 mL) black peppercorns, crushed
- 1 tablespoon (15 mL) juniper berries, crushed
- 1½ lb (675 g) boneless pork belly, skin removed

BRAISING THE PORK BELLY

- 1/4 cup (60 mL) canola oil
- 1 medium carrot, coarsely chopped
- 1 celery rib, coarsely chopped
- 1 onion, coarsely chopped
- 1 fennel bulb, quartered
- 2 garlic cloves, crushed
- 4 cups (1 L) veal stock
- 1 cup (250 mL) old-fashioned or unfiltered apple juice
- 2 sprigs of thyme

COFFEE GLAZE

- 2 cups (500 mL) braising liquid
- 1 tablespoon (15 mL) freshly brewed espresso
- 1 tablespoon (15 mL) cider vinegar
- 1 teaspoon (5 mL) honey

SCALLOPS

- 1 tablespoon (15 mL) canola oil (if needed)
- 6 large sea scallops
- Maldon sea salt and freshly cracked black pepper

TO CURE THE PORK BELLY:

In a bowl, stir together the salt, brown sugar, peppercorns, and juniper berries. Rub the pork belly all over with the salt mixture. Cover and refrigerate for 12 hours.

TO BRAISE THE PORK BELLY:

Preheat oven to 350°F (180°C).

Wipe the salt mixture off the pork belly. In a large, heavy pot, heat 2 tablespoons (30 mL) of the canola oil over medium-high heat. Sear the pork belly on all sides, about 5 minutes. Add the carrot, celery, onion, fennel, and garlic; continue cooking, stirring frequently, for another 5 minutes or until the vegetables are caramelized.

Add the veal stock, apple juice, and thyme. Cover with a lid or foil, transfer to the oven, and braise the pork belly for 3 hours or until tender.

Transfer the pork belly to a cutting board and set aside to cool. Meanwhile, strain the braising liquid through a large sieve set over a bowl. Discard the solids and skim the excess fat from the braising liquid. Set aside 2 cups (500 mL).

FOR THE GLAZE:

Boil the braising liquid until reduced to 1 cup (250 mL), about 15 minutes. Add the espresso, vinegar, and honey; continue cooking until the sauce is thick enough to coat the back of a spoon, about 5 minutes. Keep warm.

FINISHING THE PORK BELLY:

Cut the pork belly into large cubes. Heat the remaining 2 tablespoons (30 mL) canola oil in a large skillet over high heat. Sear the pork belly on all sides until crispy, about 3 minutes. Remove from the pan and keep warm.

FOR THE SCALLOPS:

Season the scallops with salt and pepper. Add canola oil to the skillet if necessary; heat over high heat. Sear the scallops for 1 minute. Turn off the heat, flip the scallops, and let sit for another minute.

To serve, divide the pork belly among warm plates. Spoon the coffee glaze over the pork belly. Top each serving with a scallop. Season with sea salt and cracked pepper.

COOK'S NOTE:

The pork belly can be braised a day ahead. Leave it in the braising liquid to cool, then cover and place in the refrigerator.

BLACK COD RATATOUILLE WITH HERB SALAD

PREP 30 MIN × COOK 20 MIN × SERVES 4

This recipe is a stunner. Not only does it look incredible in its papillote package, it tastes even better. By wrapping it in parchment paper, you steam the fish in its own juices, keeping it flavourful and moist. If you can't find black cod, any white fish will do.

BLACK COD RATATOUILLE
- 1 onion, thinly sliced
- 2 Japanese or baby eggplants, thinly sliced
- 1 zucchini, thinly sliced
- 1 summer squash, thinly sliced
- 1 tomato, thinly sliced
- Maldon sea salt and freshly cracked black pepper
- 1 black cod fillet (2 lb/900 g), skinned
- 2 tablespoons (30 mL) olive oil
- 1 red bell pepper, diced
- 1 garlic clove, minced
- 4 sprigs of thyme
- 2 tablespoons (30 mL) butter, cubed

HERB SALAD
- Leaves from a bunch of basil
- Leaves from a bunch of parsley
- Leaves from a bunch of celery
- Leaves from a bunch of chervil
- Sprigs from a bunch of dill, coarsely chopped
- A bunch of chives, cut in 1-inch (2.5 cm) pieces
- 1 teaspoon (5 mL) white balsamic vinegar
- 1 teaspoon (5 mL) olive oil
- Salt and freshly cracked black pepper

FOR THE BLACK COD RATATOUILLE:
Preheat oven to 400°F (200°C).

Cover a baking sheet with a piece of parchment paper about 2 inches (5 cm) wider than the tray on each side. In the centre of the parchment, arrange alternating slices of onion, eggplant, zucchini, summer squash, and tomato, closely overlapping, making a layer roughly the size of the fish. Season the vegetables with Maldon salt and pepper. Lay the black cod on top of the vegetables. Drizzle with olive oil. Garnish with the red pepper, garlic, and thyme. Season with salt and pepper. Dot with the butter.

Bring up each long side of the parchment paper to the centre and make a small fold to join them. Continue folding down the parchment, creating a tight seal. Crimp the short ends and twist to seal the fish and ratatouille inside.

Bake for about 20 minutes, until the fish is flaky.

FOR THE HERB SALAD:
While the fish is baking, in a large bowl, toss together the basil, parsley, celery leaves, chervil, dill, and chives. Add the vinegar and olive oil; toss again. Season with salt and pepper.

To serve, transfer the papillote to a platter. With a knife, cut the paper to reveal the fish. Garnish the fish with the herb salad.

AFFOGATO

PREP 5 MIN × SERVES 4

This is the easiest dessert ever. All you need is strong espresso and a good-quality ice cream for the perfect after-dinner coffee treat.

- Zest and juice of 1 lemon
- 1 tablespoon (15 mL) sugar
- 4 small scoops of good-quality vanilla ice cream
- 1 cup (250 mL) freshly brewed strong espresso

Rim the edges of 4 espresso cups with lemon juice and then sugar. Scoop a generous serving of ice cream into each cup. Top with lemon zest and a shot of espresso.

Serve with Dark Chocolate, Espresso, and Pistachio Biscotti (page 80).

DARK CHOCOLATE, ESPRESSO, AND PISTACHIO BISCOTTI

PREP 20 MIN PLUS 30 MIN FOR CHILLING × COOK 50 MIN × MAKES 12 BISCOTTI

Because I use dark chocolate here, these biscotti are a perfect semisweet match for my affogato dessert, or on their own with coffee or tea.

- 2 cups (500 mL) all-purpose flour
- 1/2 cup (125 mL) cocoa powder, sifted
- 2 tablespoons (30 mL) finely ground coffee
- 1 teaspoon (5 mL) baking soda
- 1/2 teaspoon (2 mL) salt
- 1 cup (250 mL) sugar
- 1/3 cup (75 mL) butter, softened
- 2 teaspoons (10 mL) vanilla extract
- 2 large eggs
- Zest of 1 lemon
- 1 cup (250 mL) shelled unsalted pistachios, toasted
- 1/2 cup (125 mL) finely chopped semisweet chocolate

Line a baking sheet with parchment paper.

In a medium bowl, mix together the flour, cocoa powder, ground coffee, baking soda, and salt.

In a large bowl with an electric mixer, cream the sugar, butter, and vanilla until smooth. Add the eggs; beat until well combined and creamy, scraping down the sides of the bowl if necessary. Add the lemon zest and flour mixture; stir to form a stiff dough. Stir in the pistachios and chopped chocolate.

Transfer the dough to the prepared baking sheet and shape it into a slightly flattened log, about 12 inches (30 cm) long and 4 inches (10 cm) wide. Cover loosely with plastic wrap and refrigerate for 30 minutes or until firm.

Preheat oven to 350°F (180°C). Bake log until slightly firm, about 35 minutes. Cool on the baking sheet for 15 minutes. Reduce oven temperature to 300°F (150°C).

On a cutting board, and using a sharp serrated knife, cut the log diagonally into 1/2-inch (1 cm) slices. Return the biscotti, cut sides down, to the baking sheet. Bake until crisp, about 15 minutes. Cool on racks.

Serve with Affogato (page 78) if desired.

THE WINE GUYS

White Wine Spritzer

Spinach and Lemon Risotto with Ouzo Shrimp

Sabayon with Fresh Cherries and Granola Pecan Bars

The beauty of my relationship with my business partners is that each one of us has a particular strength. I'm in charge of the food and kitchen, Tim is an incredible bartender, shucker, and the creator of all our restaurant playlists, and Kyle is in charge of the wine and the front of house—a.k.a. "the boss."

For Kyle and me, the dynamic was pretty much the same back when I was twenty-three, Kyle was nineteen, and we were both working at Globe. I was in the kitchen and Kyle was behind the bar. We were both young, having a good time, and starting out in the restaurant world with no clue that we would still be doing this together more than ten years later.

While my passion for food grew, Kyle became fascinated with the world of wine. Wine is essential to our business, and in an area that can be a bit snobby and elitist, having someone in charge who's as down to earth about wine as Kyle makes the whole experience all the more approachable. Kyle is constantly learning about new producers and different techniques, always tasting, and always teaching the staff everything he knows. And because he knows so much, I'm going to let him tell you about what goes on with the wine side of things at the restaurant.

Wine is pretty much the best thing ever created and plays a huge role in the culinary world. For me and my personal dining choices, it's 50 per cent of the experience. I love wine alone, I love it as a pairing tool to make food even better, and I love how food can also make the wine itself better.

Our wine list is relatively extensive, with about 120 red and around 60 white selections. We have a lot of options from France and Italy, the traditional wine-growing regions, as well selections from around the world. But we're definitely open minded. If I taste a good wine, I'm going to put it on the list regardless of where it's from.

We tend to have a fairly seafood-heavy menu, so we need to have a nice balance and a good selection of white wine while also acknowledging that a lot of people are into red no matter the food. In that case we look for slightly more delicate red wines, or reds that have less tannic structure. But I think that our overall philosophy is that people should get to drink what they want. Wine is about taste—what's important is that the customer likes what they're drinking. If they want to drink a Californian Cabernet with a seafood platter, I'd never recommend it as a pairing, but if that's what makes them happy, go for it.

It's really important to me that the staff be knowledgeable about wines, and it's something that I promote as much as possible. It can only make the diner's experience better. We've recently started a wine series where every two weeks we try a set of wines from a certain region or a certain grape, blind. This allows us to be able to do two things: one, learn about the wines on our list, and two, learn about the general characteristics of that region or grape.

Wine does not have to be that complicated. You *can* be complicated about it—there's a million things we could talk about: pH levels, vinification techniques, soil type, vineyard classification, vine age, or the producer—and for some people that's really important. But for me, at our restaurant, despite all those things that I find interesting, the most important thing is that the wine tastes great. It's what is in the glass that counts.

Every month our wine supplier, Theo from the Montreal wine agency Œnopole, comes by with bottles for Kyle to taste. Theo is an extremely involved, diehard food-and-wine guy. Every conversation with him is about what he's cooking and what he's pairing his food with that night.

Just like Kyle, Theo is one of those guys who brings enthusiasm to his business and is totally engrossed in what he does. Kyle and I work with Theo because his involvement is contagious, and it helps us bring that energy to our staff and customers. Normally I don't talk to wine guys because I don't drink, and without actually tasting what they're going on about, the conversation can be a bit . . . uninteresting. But Theo is different. He gets me excited for other reasons, whether it's a food angle, a tidbit about the wine's history or the winemaker or a regional quirk—anything like that piques my interest. That's how I remember wines—by stories, not taste—and it's this quality that Theo brings to the table. He's not just another agent blabbing on about this and that; he has a way of taking it down a notch and making wine more approachable and real. And to get a guy like me who doesn't even touch the stuff interested is a pretty awesome feat.

Having a partner like Kyle who brings different qualities and interests to Garde Manger helps us complement each other. Just like I would never trust Kyle cooking on the line, I don't think he'd let me pick out a wine because he knows I'd just go for the nicest-looking label or the best story.

WHITE WINE SPRITZER

PREP 5 MIN × SERVES 1

Nothing says refreshing on a hot summer day like a white wine spritzer with fresh fruit. If you're like me and you don't drink, try this spritzer with apple champagne and ginger ale.

- 6 strawberries, hulled and halved
- 4 oz (125 mL) Riesling or other crisp white wine, chilled
- 2 oz (60 mL) club soda, ginger ale, flavoured sparkling water, or apple champagne
- Blueberries and sliced peaches for garnish

In a jar, combine the strawberries with the wine. Cover and refrigerate overnight.

Pour into a glass, top with club soda, and garnish with a couple of blueberries and peach slices.

....

COOK'S NOTE:
Apple champagne is my favourite non-alcoholic drink. It's made with the traditional méthode champenoise process and is available in white or rosé. You can find it in Montreal at Les Douceurs du Marché. Sparkling apple cider is a good substitute.

....

SPINACH AND LEMON RISOTTO WITH OUZO SHRIMP

PREP 10 MIN × COOK 35 MIN × SERVES 4

This dish works as either a starter or a main course, and it really brings together some simple ingredients. A splash of ouzo provides just a hint of anise at the end—the perfect Greek flair.

RISOTTO

- 4 cups (1 L) chicken or vegetable stock
- 1 onion, finely chopped
- 1 tablespoon (15 mL) olive oil
- 2 cups (500 mL) arborio rice
- 1/4 cup (60 mL) butter
- 1 cup (250 mL) grated kefalotyri cheese (4 oz/115 g)
- 1 cup (250 mL) crumbled feta cheese (4 oz/115 g), plus more for garnish
- 4 cups (1 L) baby spinach
- Zest and juice of 1 lemon
- Salt and freshly cracked black pepper

OUZO SHRIMP

- 1 tablespoon (15 mL) canola oil
- 12 large shrimp, peeled (tail shells left intact) and deveined
- 2 tablespoons (30 mL) ouzo
- 2 tablespoons (30 mL) butter
- Salt and freshly cracked black pepper

PARSLEY SALAD

- 1/4 cup (60 mL) chopped fresh parsley
- A drizzle of extra-virgin olive oil
- Zest of 1 lemon
- Maldon sea salt and freshly cracked black pepper

FOR THE RISOTTO:

In a saucepan, bring the stock to a simmer over medium-low heat.

In a large saucepan, cook the onion in the olive oil over medium-low heat, stirring, until softened, about 5 minutes. Add the rice, stirring until each grain is coated with oil. Add about 3/4 cup (175 mL) simmering stock and cook over medium-high heat, stirring constantly, until the stock is absorbed. Continue adding stock, a ladle at a time, stirring constantly and letting each batch be absorbed before adding the next, until about half the stock has been used. Reduce heat if necessary to keep the risotto at a simmer. Continue adding the stock in the same manner until the rice is tender and creamy looking but still al dente, about 20 minutes.

Reduce heat to low. Stir in the butter, then the kefalotyri and feta. Mix well. Stir in the spinach and lemon zest and juice. Season with salt and pepper. Remove from heat and keep warm.

FOR THE OUZO SHRIMP:

In a heavy skillet, heat the oil over medium-high heat. Sauté the shrimp for 2 to 3 minutes. Take the pan off the heat, immediately add the ouzo, and carefully light it. As soon as the flames go out, put the pan back on the heat and swirl in the butter. Season with salt and pepper. Set aside.

FOR THE PARSLEY SALAD:

In a small bowl, stir together the parsley, olive oil, and lemon zest. Season with salt and pepper.

To serve, spoon the risotto onto warm plates. Garnish each serving with shrimp and the parsley salad.

COOK'S NOTE:

Kefalotyri is a Greek hard cheese made from sheep or goat's milk. You can substitute Romano, pecorino, or Parmesan cheese.

SABAYON WITH FRESH CHERRIES & GRANOLA PECAN BARS

Sabayon is a light custard made with whipped egg yolks and usually flavoured with an alcohol like Marsala or champagne. Here I use a non-alcoholic sparkling apple cider that lends itself nicely to the fruit and nut bars.

SABAYON WITH FRESH CHERRIES

PREP 10 MIN × COOK 4 MIN × SERVES 4

- 6 large egg yolks
- 1 cup (250 mL) apple champagne
- 1/3 cup (75 mL) sugar
- Seeds scraped from 1 vanilla bean
- A dash of lemon juice
- Fresh cherries, pitted

Pour a few inches of water into a large saucepan and place over medium heat.

In a heatproof bowl, whisk together the egg yolks, apple champagne, sugar, and vanilla seeds. Place the bowl over the saucepan of hot (not simmering) water. Cook for 4 to 5 minutes, whisking constantly and adjusting the heat as needed, or until the sabayon has the consistency of lightly whipped cream. Clear the bottom of the bowl constantly with the whisk so that the eggs do not scramble. Taste, and whisk in drops of lemon juice or pinches of sugar as needed. When the sabayon has thickened and tripled in volume, remove from heat.

If you wish to eat the sabayon cold, place the bowl in a larger bowl of ice cubes to chill it.

To serve, spoon cherries into individual glasses and top with sabayon. Serve with Granola Pecan Bars.

GRANOLA PECAN BARS

PREP 10 MIN × COOK 35 MIN × MAKES 18 BARS

- 2 cups (500 mL) old-fashioned rolled oats
- 1½ cups (375 mL) bran cereal
- 1 cup (250 mL) ground almonds
- 1 cup (250 mL) pecans, toasted and chopped
- 1 cup (250 mL) brown sugar
- 1 teaspoon (5 mL) cinnamon
- 1/2 teaspoon (2 mL) nutmeg
- 1/2 teaspoon (2 mL) salt
- 1/2 cup (125 mL) maple syrup
- 1/2 cup (125 mL) butter
- 2 teaspoons (10 mL) vanilla extract
- 1 large egg, beaten

Preheat oven to 350°F (180°C). Butter a 9-inch (2.5 L) square cake pan and line with parchment paper, leaving an overhang on two sides, as handles.

In a large bowl, toss together the oats, bran cereal, ground almonds, pecans, brown sugar, cinnamon, nutmeg, and salt. In a small saucepan over medium-low heat, stir the maple syrup and butter until melted. Stir in the vanilla.

Pour the syrup mixture over the oat mixture; stir until blended. Stir in the egg. Pat the granola mixture evenly into the bottom of the prepared pan. Bake for 30 minutes or until golden brown. Let cool.

Lift the granola out of the pan with parchment paper and cut into bars.

THE
LINEN GUY

PAN-SEARED BEEF CARPACCIO WITH POTATO CHIPS, FRIED CAPERS, AND LEMON AÏOLI
SPAGHETTI WITH ROASTED TOMATO SAUCE AND MEATBALLS
STICKY FIG PUDDING

I'm a neat freak. I need to have a tidy, organized restaurant or else I can't function properly. When I'm working, I always have a dishrag in my hand and I'm constantly cleaning up. Rags are similar to tea towels, and we use them for everything. An essential part of making this possible is our regular linen deliveries.

Metro Linen is our supplier, and this cool guy named Norm has been delivering our linen ever since we opened. He shows up on Tuesdays and Fridays to take our dirty linens and replace them with clean ones. Without Norm, our tables wouldn't have their crisp white cloths, our customers would have nothing to wipe their mouths or cover their laps with, and the kitchen would be a disaster zone! So when Norm walks through that door, he's everyone's best friend.

We probably go through about fifty tablecloths, over a hundred napkins, and I don't even want to know how many rags every service. Each night the floor staff not only have to make sure all the linens are folded and ready to go, but they also need rags to polish plates, silverware, and glasses and to wipe tables so everything is spic and span for the customers.

Just as the floor staff can't set up the restaurant without their linens, the kitchen staff need dishrags so that everything can run smoothly. For those who cook on the line, rags are as essential as sharp knives. Where you would use potholders or oven mitts at home, in a commercial kitchen we use our rags. Instead of using a sponge to wipe plates or countertops, we use our rags. You always want to have one rag that's dry, to protect you from heat, and one that's a bit damp, for cleaning. But don't mix them up, because if

you grab a hot pan out of the oven with a damp rag, you'll never do it again!

When I started cooking in this business we were given two rags at the beginning of the night and that was it. If we lost one, tough luck, and it usually meant we were going to have the worst shift ever. I'm a bit more lenient with my staff, but we still tend to have a supply problem since we go through too many. I actually keep a secret stash where I know no one will look. (Just in case any of my kitchen staff are reading this, you'll never find it!) And when we actually do run out of rags during service? I can't tell you how many times I've washed batches in the dishwasher and dried them in the oven!

Without Norm and his fresh linen, Garde Manger would not be the clean, organized, functioning place it is. So when Norm arrives at the restaurant, he gets whatever he wants.

PAN-SEARED BEEF CARPACCIO

WITH POTATO CHIPS, FRIED CAPERS, AND LEMON AÏOLI

PREP 30 MIN × COOK 10 MIN × SERVES 4

PAN-SEARED BEEF CARPACCIO

- 1 tablespoon (15 mL) crushed coriander seeds
- 1 tablespoon (15 mL) crushed cumin seeds
- 1 tablespoon (15 mL) crushed mustard seeds
- 1 tablespoon (15 mL) kosher salt
- 1 tablespoon (15 mL) crushed black pepper
- 1 beef tenderloin roast (1½ lb/675 g)
- 2 tablespoons (30 mL) canola oil

LEMON AÏOLI

- 1 garlic clove
- 1 teaspoon (5 mL) kosher salt
- 1 large egg
- 1 teaspoon (5 mL) Dijon mustard
- 1 cup (250 mL) olive oil
- Zest and juice of 1/2 lemon
- Salt and freshly cracked black pepper

POTATO CHIPS AND FRIED CAPERS

- 2 or 3 Yukon Gold potatoes, peeled and very thinly sliced
- 1/4 cup (60 mL) small capers, drained
- Canola oil for deep-frying
- Maldon sea salt

GARNISH

- 4 cups (1 L) mâche
- 3 tablespoons (45 mL) extra-virgin olive oil
- 2 tablespoons (30 mL) white balsamic vinegar
- Maldon sea salt and freshly cracked black pepper
- 2 tablespoons (30 mL) minced fresh chives

FOR THE BEEF CARPACCIO:

In a small bowl, stir together the coriander, cumin, mustard seeds, salt, and pepper. Rub the spice mix all over the beef. In a heavy skillet, heat the oil over medium-high heat. Sear the beef until golden brown and crusted on all sides, about 2 minutes on each side.

Wrap the beef in plastic wrap and refrigerate for about 20 minutes to make it easier to slice.

FOR THE LEMON AÏOLI:

With the side of a knife, crush the garlic. Sprinkle the salt over it. Using the side of the knife, gradually work the salt into the garlic to make a paste. In a small bowl, whisk together the egg and mustard. Whisk in the garlic paste. Slowly whisk in the oil, a little at a time, until all the oil is used and the aïoli is emulsified. Add lemon zest and juice. If you need to thin the sauce, whisk in water, a few drops at a time, until you get the consistency you like. Season with salt and pepper. Cover and keep refrigerated until ready to use. (Use within 24 hours.)

FOR THE POTATO CHIPS AND FRIED CAPERS:

Rinse the potato slices under cold water until the water runs clear. Drain the potatoes and pat dry between paper towels. Pat dry the capers between paper towels.

In a deep-fryer or deep, heavy saucepan, heat 2 inches (5 cm) of canola oil to 350°F (180°C). Working in small batches, fry the potato chips, stirring a few times, until golden, about 2 minutes. Transfer to paper towels to drain. Sprinkle with Maldon salt.

Fry the capers until golden, 30 to 45 seconds. Drain on paper towels.

FOR THE GARNISH:

In a bowl, toss the mâche with olive oil and vinegar. Season with salt and pepper.

To serve, unwrap the beef. Using a very sharp knife, cut slices as thin as you can. Arrange the beef on individual plates. Spoon the lemon aïoli on the beef. Garnish with the mâche, potato chips, fried capers, and chives.

COOK'S NOTES:

Rinsing the potatoes removes some of the starch, making for crispier chips.

Aïoli is also great on burgers and sandwiches, and as a dip for vegetables.

SPAGHETTI WITH ROASTED TOMATO SAUCE AND MEATBALLS

PREP 30 MIN × COOK 1½ HOURS × SERVES 4

I know, I know, there are a million different ways to make this dish and everyone loves their mom's the most. Once you try my roasted tomato sauce, though, you might have to make some extra room at the dinner table.

ROASTED TOMATO SAUCE
- About 8 ripe Roma tomatoes, halved lengthwise
- 2 onions, peeled and quartered
- 3 tablespoons (45 mL) olive oil
- 2 tablespoons (30 mL) icing sugar
- Coarse salt and freshly cracked black pepper
- 1 head of garlic, top sliced off to expose the cloves
- A handful of fresh basil leaves, torn

MEATBALLS
- 1/2 cup (125 mL) fresh bread crumbs
- 1/4 cup (60 mL) milk
- 1 lb (450 g) ground pork
- 1 lb (450 g) ground veal
- 1 lb (450 g) ground beef
- 1 shallot, minced
- 2 garlic cloves, minced
- Leaves from a bunch of oregano, chopped
- Leaves from a bunch of basil, chopped
- A bunch of chives, chopped
- 1/2 cup (125 mL) grated pecorino or Parmigiano-Reggiano cheese
- 3 tablespoons (45 mL) Dijon mustard
- 1 tablespoon (15 mL) paprika
- 1/2 teaspoon (2 mL) cayenne pepper
- Coarse salt and freshly cracked black pepper
- A drizzle of olive oil

FOR SERVING
- 1 lb (450 g) spaghetti
- 1 cup (250 mL) grated Parmigiano-Reggiano cheese
- Leaves from a bunch of parsley, chopped
- A bunch of chives, finely chopped

FOR THE ROASTED TOMATO SAUCE:
Preheat oven to 350°F (180°C). Line a baking sheet with parchment paper.

Spread the tomatoes cut side down on the baking sheet. (You may need to use 2 baking sheets if they don't fit in a single layer.) Add the onions. Drizzle with 2 tablespoons (30 mL) of the olive oil. Sprinkle with the icing sugar and salt and pepper. Roast for about 1 hour, until the tomatoes are soft and slightly charred in places. When cool enough to handle, remove the skins.

Meanwhile, place the garlic on a square of foil. Drizzle with the remaining 1 tablespoon (15 mL) olive oil; season with salt and pepper. Tightly wrap the garlic in the foil. Roast for about 30 minutes, until the garlic is soft throughout and nicely browned. Squeeze the garlic from the skins.

Scrape the tomatoes, onions, and their juices from the baking sheet into a blender. Add the basil leaves and roasted garlic. Blend until smooth. Transfer to a large saucepan and set aside. (*Sauce can be cooled and refrigerated, covered, for up to 4 days, or frozen.*)

FOR THE MEATBALLS:
Preheat oven to 350°F (180°C). Line a baking sheet with parchment paper.

In a large bowl, soak the bread crumbs in the milk for 10 minutes. Add the ground meat and gently mix with your hands. Add the shallot, garlic, oregano, basil, chives, pecorino, mustard, paprika, cayenne, and salt and black pepper to taste. Shape the mixture into about 50 small meatballs, arranging them on the baking sheet. Drizzle with a little olive oil. Bake for 30 minutes or until cooked through.

While the meatballs are baking, reheat the sauce and cook the spaghetti until al dente.

To serve, add the meatballs and pasta to the sauce; fold to mix. Serve sprinkled with Parmigiano-Reggiano, parsley, and chives.

STICKY FIG PUDDING

PREP 30 MIN × COOK 80 MIN × SERVES 8

Figs are one of my favourite snacks, but in this dessert, they're just decadent. Here I mix them with a warm, gooey pudding-like cake, topped off with a sprinkle of pecans and a drizzle of toffee sauce. Oh, and a scoop of vanilla ice cream for good measure.

FIG PUDDING

- **2 cups (500 mL) tender dried figs (about 20), stems removed, coarsely chopped**
- **2 cinnamon sticks (4 inches/ 10 cm each)**
- **2 cups (500 mL) water**
- **2 teaspoons (10 mL) baking soda**
- **1/2 cup (125 mL) butter, softened**
- **2 cups (500 mL) brown sugar**
- **1 teaspoon (5 mL) vanilla extract**
- **2 large eggs**
- **1½ cups (375 mL) all-purpose flour**
- **1 teaspoon (5 mL) baking powder**
- **1 teaspoon (5 mL) baking soda**
- **1/2 teaspoon (2 mL) salt**
- **1 cup (250 mL) toasted pecans, coarsely chopped**
- **Maldon sea salt**

TOFFEE SAUCE

- **1/2 cup (125 mL) butter**
- **2 cups (500 mL) brown sugar**
- **2 cups (500 mL) whipping cream**
- **1 teaspoon (5 mL) vanilla extract**

FOR THE FIG PUDDING:

Preheat oven to 350°F (180°C). Butter an 11- × 7-inch (2 L) baking dish.

In a medium saucepan, bring the figs, cinnamon sticks, and water to a boil; reduce heat and simmer for 15 minutes or until almost all the liquid has evaporated. Remove from heat. Discard the cinnamon sticks. Stir in the baking soda. Let cool.

In a large bowl with an electric mixer, beat the softened butter with the brown sugar and vanilla for 2 minutes or until the mixture is creamy. Beat in the eggs, one at a time, scraping down the sides of the bowl after each addition, and continue beating until the mixture is light, about 3 minutes. Stir in the fig mixture.

In another bowl, whisk together the flour, baking powder, baking soda, and salt. Add the flour mixture to the fig mixture. Stir just until

the batter is smooth. Scrape the batter into the prepared baking dish. Sprinkle with pecans and Maldon salt. Bake for 50 to 60 minutes or until the pudding is springy to the touch and a toothpick inserted in the centre comes out clean.

FOR THE TOFFEE SAUCE:

While the pudding is baking, in a medium saucepan, melt the butter over medium heat. Stir in the brown sugar. Cook, stirring frequently, for 5 minutes. Add the cream; bring to a boil, stirring occasionally, until the sauce starts to thicken, 10 to 15 minutes. Stir in the vanilla. Remove from heat and keep warm.

To finish the pudding, using a fork, poke holes all over the top of the warm pudding. Drizzle with half of the warm toffee sauce. Return the pudding to the oven and bake for 5 minutes or until the toffee sauce is bubbling around the edges but not fully absorbed.

Serve the fig pudding warm with the remaining toffee sauce and ice cream.

INDUSTRY

Working in the restaurant industry is far from the glamorous life some may imagine. It's long hours of hard, exhausting work. It doesn't often pay well, and it's incredibly difficult to make a lifelong career of it. We're busy at work when most people are out having fun, and we work holidays and weekends. It's hard for us to find time to see our families and even harder to take vacations. We're constantly on our feet and most of the time we eat standing up and while doing something else. Some of us drink too much and smoke too much to deal with the pressure, and some of us definitely party too much. And until we finally get to the point of running our own restaurant, we eat a lot of crap along the way.

But . . .

At the same time it's an industry full of incredibly talented, amazing people, and I don't regret the path I chose, not for a second. As much as the work is hard, it's also a lot of fun, and as much as people say the pay sucks, I've seen wait staff put themselves through university with tips and cooks put down payments on houses with their salaries. We get used to the hours, and our weekends become Sundays and Mondays. We know how to have a good time (we're usually the life of the party!), and we definitely appreciate the pleasures of food and drink. We can basically find work in any city or country because the hospitality world is universal. And for every bad night, horrible customer, or total disaster, there are ten times as many good nights, extraordinary customers, and unforgettable experiences.

For those of you who work in the industry, I hope this will remind you why you do what you do. For those who have never gone the hospitality way, I hope this helps you to better appreciate the hard work, dedication, and talent that go into your restaurant experience.

I've had an incredible time in this wild and crazy world, and I still love it. I may not be in the kitchen as much as I used to be, but anyone who knows me knows that I love getting my hands dirty. To all the hard-working people in the hospitality industry, and especially those who have taught me, guided me, scolded me, and helped me get to where I am today—my mentors, my kitchen staff, the people who have influenced my cooking, my oyster shuckers, my floor staff, my bartenders, and even the hotel concierges—I'm so lucky to be in such good company.

THE

MENTORS

CHINATOWN STEAMED OYSTERS

QUAIL AND EGG ON CREAMED SPINACH

PORTERHOUSE STEAK WITH ASPARAGUS AND HOLLANDAISE SAUCE

I was eighteen when I first worked in the restaurant business. I was a busboy, basically the bottom rank, at a hotel in Banff, Alberta, for the summer. I remember seeing all the chefs in their tall white hats who commanded total respect from all the restaurant staff. It was a whole new world I had never known about, and I knew I wanted to be part of it. When I got back to Montreal, I went into Globe, one of the city's hottest restaurants at the time, and begged for a job. They took one look at me—with my shoulder-length hair, my Birkenstocks, and a Mountain Equipment Co-op fanny pack—and told me to get a haircut, burn the fanny pack, and come back the next week to start as a busboy.

I'd been at Globe for two or three months when Dave came in as the head chef and completely changed how I saw cooking. He was big, tall, and intimidating. He didn't wear one of those white hats, and his style of cooking was raw and real. I knew right away we were cut from the same cloth, and I realized that a guy like me could be taken seriously in this industry. I hadn't wanted to be a chef particularly, but after watching Dave killing it in the kitchen night after night, I knew this was the job for me.

Watching Dave work made me decide to go to cooking school and see what it was all about. After my first day of classes, I was totally hooked. By the time I returned to Globe to do my internship, Dave had become the executive chef and Fred was the head chef. Just like with Dave, I had an instant connection with Fred. The man is a genius, and he was doing amazing things that blew my mind. We had a crazy time together where we never slept, just worked and worked making incredible food that we thought was going to change the world.

Dave and Fred were ahead of their time in how they approached cooking. Their passion for food fed my own, and they opened my eyes to a new way of doing things. They taught me to look beyond each dish, read everything, watch closely, and most important, follow my instincts. It was less the actual cooking and more the philosophy behind the food that began to define the chef I wanted to become.

Since those early days, I've had the opportunity to meet chefs from all over the world, and whether they were working in a makeshift kitchen or in a Michelin-starred restaurant, they've all contributed to how I cook today. I think it's important to learn to appreciate each ingredient, each individual technique, and each person's drive, regardless of who they are and where they cook, and allow these things to influence my own approach.

Dave and Fred eventually became business partners, and about a year before I opened Garde Manger, they opened Joe Beef, now a Montreal institution. A lot has changed, but a lot has also stayed the same. Although we've ended up as competitors, I have the ultimate respect for them, their success, and how they stay true to their roots.

CHINATOWN STEAMED OYSTERS

PREP 10 MIN × COOK 1 MIN × SERVES 4

When I worked with Dave and Fred, if we were hungry after our shift we'd head over to Chinatown for these giant steamed oysters late at night. This is my own version, dedicated to them.

SAUCE

- 1/4 cup (60 mL) soy sauce
- 1 tablespoon (15 mL) finely chopped lemongrass
- 1 teaspoon (5 mL) honey
- 1 teaspoon (5 mL) Sriracha hot sauce
- Zest and juice of 1 lime

STEAMED OYSTERS

- 12 large Pacific Coast oysters, shucked (page 135), bottom shells and liquor reserved
- 3 garlic cloves, minced
- 2 green onions, chopped

FOR THE SAUCE:

In a medium bowl, whisk together the soy sauce, lemongrass, honey, Sriracha, lime zest and juice, and reserved oyster liquor.

FOR THE STEAMED OYSTERS:

Bring about an inch (2.5 cm) of water to a boil in a wok. Place the oysters back in their bottom shells and arrange in a large bamboo steamer. Sprinkle the oysters with garlic. Cover the steamer, set it in the wok, and steam the oysters for 1 to 2 minutes.

Transfer the steamer to a serving plate. Spoon the sauce over the oysters and sprinkle with chopped green onions.

QUAIL AND EGG ON CREAMED SPINACH

PREP 25 MIN × COOK 25 MIN × SERVES 4

I like to make this recipe when I want to show off a bit, but it's really easy to make and will definitely impress your dinner guests when the soft-boiled egg breaks and the yolk melts into the dish—perfection!

FRIED EGGS

- 6 large eggs
- 1/2 cup (125 mL) all-purpose flour
- Salt and freshly cracked black pepper
- 1/2 cup (125 mL) dry bread crumbs
- Canola oil for deep-frying

CREAMED SPINACH

- 2 lb (900 g) fresh spinach, tough stems removed
- 1 cup (250 mL) whipping cream
- 1 tablespoon (15 mL) Dijon mustard
- 2 tablespoons (30 mL) butter
- 1 shallot, finely chopped
- 1 garlic clove, minced
- Salt and freshly cracked black pepper

QUAIL

- 4 quail
- Salt and freshly cracked black pepper
- 1 tablespoon (15 mL) canola oil

HERB GARNISH

- Leaves from 6 sprigs of flat-leaf parsley, chopped
- Leaves from 2 sprigs of basil, chopped
- Leaves from 2 sprigs of thyme

- 1 garlic clove, minced
- 2 tablespoons (30 mL) olive oil
- Maldon sea salt and freshly cracked black pepper

FOR THE FRIED EGGS:

Boil 4 of the eggs for 5 minutes for soft-boiled. Drain and cool in ice-cold water. Peel the eggs.

Put the flour in a shallow dish and season with salt and pepper. Put the bread crumbs in a second dish. In a third dish, lightly beat the remaining 2 eggs.

Dredge the boiled eggs in the flour, then in the egg, and finally in the bread crumbs, coating thoroughly. Transfer to a plate and refrigerate.

FOR THE CREAMED SPINACH:

Bring a pot of salted water to a boil over high heat. Add the spinach and cook for 15 seconds. Drain in a fine-mesh strainer, pressing with a large spoon to release as much water as possible.

In a small saucepan, simmer the cream until reduced by half, about 10 minutes. Stir in the mustard. Set aside.

Melt the butter in a medium skillet over medium-high heat. Add the shallot and garlic; cook, stirring, until soft and fragrant, about 2 minutes. Add the spinach; cook, stirring, just until the liquid is released. Stir in the reduced cream mixture. Season with salt and

pepper. Remove from heat and keep warm.

FOR THE QUAIL:

Preheat oven to 350°F (180°C).

Using a sharp knife, slice straight through the breastbone of each quail to open the cavity. Carefully cut away and remove the rib cage so you have a boneless breast attached to the bone-in legs and wings. (If the breast breaks away from the legs, which can happen with such a small bird, cook each portion separately.)

Season the quail with salt and pepper. In a large ovenproof skillet, heat the oil over high heat. Add the quail and brown them on all sides. Finish cooking them in the oven for about 8 minutes. Cut them in half and keep warm.

FOR THE HERB GARNISH:

Shortly before serving, in a bowl, combine the parsley, basil, thyme, and garlic; toss. Add olive oil and season with Maldon salt and pepper.

TO FINISH THE EGGS:

In a deep-fryer or deep, heavy saucepan, heat 2 inches (5 cm) of canola oil to 350°F (180°C). Fry the eggs for about 1 minute or just until the crust is lightly browned. Cut the eggs in half.

To serve, divide the creamed spinach among 4 plates. Top with the quail. Garnish with the herb mixture and the fried eggs.

PORTERHOUSE STEAK WITH ASPARAGUS AND HOLLANDAISE SAUCE

PREP 15 MIN × COOK 20 MIN × SERVES 4

You don't need a grill to cook a perfect steak, but an inexpensive cast-iron pan is essential. Once you try a pan-fried steak, you'll see why so many chefs swear by it.

Asparagus with hollandaise is always a crowd pleaser, and the sauce is not as complicated as you might think. A cooking-school basic, hollandaise takes just a few simple steps and voilà!

HOLLANDAISE SAUCE
- 4 large egg yolks
- Juice of 1/2 lemon
- 1/2 cup (125 mL) butter, melted
- 1 teaspoon (5 mL) chopped fresh tarragon
- 1/2 teaspoon (2 mL) Dijon mustard
- Salt and freshly cracked black pepper

PORTERHOUSE STEAK
- 4 porterhouse steaks
- Salt and freshly cracked black pepper
- 2 tablespoons (30 mL) canola oil
- 2 tablespoons (30 mL) butter

ASPARAGUS
- 1 tablespoon (15 mL) butter
- 1 shallot, finely chopped
- 1/2 lb (225 g) asparagus, blanched
- Salt and freshly cracked black pepper

FOR THE HOLLANDAISE SAUCE:
Whisk the egg yolks and lemon juice in a heatproof bowl until the mixture is thickened, pale, and doubled in volume, about 5 minutes. Place the bowl over a saucepan containing an inch (2.5 cm) or so of barely simmering water (or use a double boiler). Continue to whisk rapidly. Be careful not to let the eggs get too hot or they will scramble. Whisking constantly, slowly drizzle the melted butter into the eggs. Continue to whisk until the sauce has thickened. Remove from heat. Whisk in the tarragon and mustard. Season with salt and pepper. Keep warm over warm water until ready to serve. If the sauce gets too thick, whisk in a few drops of warm water before serving.

FOR THE PORTERHOUSE STEAK:
Preheat oven to 350°F (180°C).

Season the steaks with salt and pepper. Heat the oil in a large, heavy ovenproof skillet (preferably cast iron) over high heat. Add the steaks and sear on both sides, 3 minutes on each side.

Place the skillet in the oven for another 6 minutes. Top each steak with some butter and cook for another 2 minutes for medium-rare.

Transfer the steaks to a warm plate and let rest for about 10 minutes, loosely covered with foil.

FOR THE ASPARAGUS:
In a large skillet, melt the butter over medium-high heat. Add the shallot and asparagus; cook, shaking the pan occasionally, for about 2 minutes. Season with salt and pepper.

To serve, place a steak on each of 4 warm plates. Divide the asparagus among the plates and top with hollandaise sauce. Serve with french fries.

KITCHEN STAFF

JALAPEÑO CRAB POPPERS
CREAMED CORN
CHEESE AND CARAMELIZED SHALLOT POPOVERS
TURDUCKEN

The kitchen staff at Garde Manger has evolved over the years, and that is a reflection of how cooking is being taken more seriously by the public. It's a new era for the food and restaurant business, and people are more interested than ever in what goes on behind the scenes. Our kitchen staff know that they can make a difference, and that has completely changed the game.

Anyone in the restaurant business will tell you the kitchen is a very transient place. That's one of the things I love about it: all the crazy characters you meet, the insane lives they lead, the partying, the moving from place to place. A lot of cooks are fuelled by the work-hard, play-hard mentality because cooking on the line is tough. The hours are long, the pressure is high, there's heat and knives, noise and fire. It takes its toll, both physically and mentally.

When we first opened, we definitely had that "go hard or go home" attitude, but things are different now. We went from a group of renegade pirates who thought they knew everything, didn't sleep at night, and acted like savage maniacs to the complete opposite: total food nerds!

Right now, for our kitchen staff, food is everything. We have a staff that cook because they love it. After work they don't go out and get wasted; they go home and practise making a perfect brunoise. They're culinary geeks who live and breathe food. They're constantly reading books about food, they're going out to dinner, they're experimenting and bringing new ideas to the table. Their passion inspires me on a daily basis.

Every day in the kitchen is a constant battle. Orders come in, dishes pile up, food has to be prepped and ready to go, plates go out on the pass, pans are in and out of the oven, night after night after night. Keeping up with that level of intensity is a real challenge—especially in the kitchen at Garde Manger, where, because of its size, there can only be three cooks on the line. We're doing 150 covers a night, and for three people to handle that is a lot of work. These cooks are put through the wringer, and they have to love it to keep on coming back for more.

One of the toughest things about this business is finding people who are the right fit and building a team. Working in the kitchen here is not just about being able to dice an onion. It's about grasping the bigger picture. It's more than just showing up. It's about stepping up and being accountable. From the dishwasher to prep cooks, the garde manger, sous-chef, and chef, we like to surround ourselves with people who always want to go above and beyond.

My own position at the restaurant has changed over the years. I used to be the guy who lived his life in the kitchen, seven days a week, eighteen hours a day. I'm still there now, but in a different way. I'm not a big fan of titles, but I guess you could say I'm the executive chef. People ask me all the time, "Don't you miss cooking every night?" And I think to myself, that's got to be someone who's never, *ever* worked on the line.

We always try to be good to our kitchen staff because after about seventeen years in the business, I know that happy workers are hard workers. We always give them two days off a week, and we encourage them to go live their lives. When people do leave us for some time off, to work in another kitchen or even another country, they learn new things and come back to us inspired.

One of the most important people to us is our head chef, James. He always steps up to the plate and gives 100 per cent every time. He's not only capable of executing the food, but he rallies the troops, day and night. He keeps everyone motivated (and a bit scared) but also happy and excited to be cooking here at Garde Manger.

The bottom line is that I could never have gotten to where I am today without the crew who battle it out in the kitchen with me. Everyone has been essential to our success, and I am grateful for all their energy and devotion.

JALAPEÑO CRAB POPPERS

PREP 20 MIN × COOK 5 MIN × SERVES 4

I know jalapeños stuffed with cheese are common on menus, but you have to try my version with crabmeat. The sweetness of the crab adds a new dimension that takes this spicy snack to the next level. Get a couple of cooked crabs, crack them open, and then pack those peppers until they're ready to pop.

FLAVOURED SOUR CREAM

- 1/2 cup (125 mL) sour cream
- 2 tablespoons (30 mL) finely chopped fresh chives
- Zest and juice of 1 lemon
- Salt and freshly cracked black pepper

JALAPEÑO CRAB POPPERS

- 4 jalapeño peppers (or milder peppers)
- 1 cup (250 mL) fresh crabmeat
- 1/2 cup (125 mL) shredded Monterey Jack cheese or preferred local cheese
- 1/2 cup (125 mL) soft goat cheese
- Salt and freshly cracked black pepper
- Canola oil for deep-frying
- 1 egg
- 1 cup (250 mL) all-purpose flour
- 1 cup (250 mL) beer

FOR THE FLAVOURED SOUR CREAM:
In a small bowl, stir together the sour cream, chives, and lemon zest and juice. Season with salt and pepper. Cover and refrigerate until using.

FOR THE JALAPEÑO CRAB POPPERS:
Carefully cut down one side of the peppers and use a small knife to remove the seeds.

In a bowl, combine the crabmeat, Monterey Jack, and goat cheese; stir to mix well. Season with salt and pepper. Stuff the jalapeño peppers with the crab mixture.

In a deep-fryer or deep, heavy saucepan, heat 2 inches (5 cm) of canola oil to 350°F (180°C).

In a medium bowl, beat the egg. Stir in the flour and beer to make a batter. Dip the peppers in the batter, coating thoroughly. Fry them for about 5 minutes or until golden brown and crispy. Drain on paper towels.

Serve the poppers with the flavoured sour cream for dipping.

CREAMED CORN

PREP 15 MIN × COOK 35 MIN × SERVES 4

When my grandmother could no longer eat corn on the cob because her dentures would fall out, we made this recipe for her. Same fresh corn flavour, but no need to chew!

- 12 ears corn, shucked
- 2 cups (500 mL) whipping cream
- 1/2 head of roasted garlic (page 150)
- 1/4 cup (60 mL) grated Parmigiano-Reggiano cheese
- 2 tablespoons (30 mL) butter
- 3 tablespoons (45 mL) minced fresh chives
- Salt and freshly cracked black pepper

Using a sharp knife and working over a bowl, scrape the corn kernels and milk from the cobs. In a large skillet, bring the cream and roasted garlic to a simmer. Add the corn and simmer for 30 minutes or until the corn is tender and the mixture is thick and creamy. Remove from heat and stir in the Parmesan, butter, and chives. Season with salt and pepper.

CHEESE <small>AND</small> CARAMELIZED SHALLOT POPOVERS

PREP 25 MIN × COOK 40 MIN × MAKES 6 POPOVERS

These variations on Yorkshire pudding are called popovers because when you bake them, they puff up over the edges of the pan. You can put practically anything in or on them, savoury or sweet.

CARAMELIZED SHALLOTS

- 2 tablespoons (30 mL) olive oil
- 3 shallots, thinly sliced
- 1 tablespoon (15 mL) chopped fresh rosemary
- Salt and freshly cracked black pepper

POPOVERS

- 2 cups (500 mL) all-purpose flour
- 1 teaspoon (5 mL) salt
- 2 cups (500 mL) milk
- 4 large eggs, at room temperature
- 2 to 3 tablespoons (30 to 45 mL) duck fat, melted
- 1 cup (250 mL) shredded sharp Cheddar cheese (4 oz/115 g)

FOR THE CARAMELIZED SHALLOTS:
In a small skillet, heat the oil over medium-high heat. Add the shallots and cook, stirring frequently, until caramelized, about 10 minutes. Stir in the rosemary. Remove from heat and season with salt and pepper.

FOR THE POPOVERS:
Position a rack in the lower third of the oven and preheat oven to 450°F (230°C).

Place a popover or muffin pan, or 6 individual custard dishes, on a baking sheet and preheat just until hot, about 10 minutes.

Meanwhile, in a large bowl, stir together the flour and salt.

In a saucepan, heat the milk over low heat for about 5 minutes.

In a medium bowl, whisk the eggs for 2 to 3 minutes, until they are very frothy. Slowly whisk in the hot milk. Add the milk mixture to the flour mixture; gently whisk just until the batter is mixed and a few small lumps remain. (Do not overmix.)

Transfer the batter to a large measuring cup or pitcher.

Remove the popover pan from the oven and pour about 1 teaspoon (5 mL) duck fat into each cup. Put the pan back in the oven until the fat is very hot but not burning, about 2 minutes. Take the pan out again and divide the batter among the cups. Top with the caramelized shallots and the cheese. Bake, without opening the oven door, for 15 minutes or until the popovers are just becoming crusty and golden brown.

Reduce oven temperature to 350°F (180°C). Continue baking for 10 minutes. Remove the pan from the oven. With a small sharp knife, pierce the top of each popover to release the steam and dry the inside of the popovers. Bake for another 5 minutes or until the popovers are puffy and golden brown and the sides are firm and crusty. Remove from oven, turn out of the pan and serve immediately. (*Popovers can be cooled on a rack, individually wrapped in plastic, and frozen. Reheat them on a baking sheet for about 10 minutes at 325°F/165°C.*)

TURDUCKEN

PREP 2 HOURS PLUS 2 HOURS RESTING FOR DOUGH × COOK 5 HOURS × SERVES 20

This has got to be the craziest, most insane recipe I've ever made. It's a chicken inside a duck inside a turkey and baked as one big, beautiful bird. It's not for cooks who don't like to get their hands dirty. It takes a bit of time and you may need a little help, but man oh man, is it one impressive dish! Did I mention it's delicious?

CORN BREAD
- 1½ cups (375 mL) warm water (110 to 115°F/43 to 46°C)
- 1 tablespoon (15 mL) sugar
- 1 tablespoon (15 mL) salt
- 2 teaspoons (10 mL) active dry yeast
- 2 cups (500 mL) all-purpose flour
- 1 cup (250 mL) corn flour
- Egg wash (2 eggs beaten with a splash of water)
- A sprinkle of coarse salt

STUFFING
- 2 tablespoons (30 mL) canola oil
- 1 lb (450 g) Morteau, Toulouse, or kielbasa sausage, casing removed, diced
- 2 celery ribs, finely chopped
- 1 onion, finely chopped
- 1 red bell pepper, finely chopped
- 4 garlic cloves, minced
- 1 cup (250 mL) veal or chicken stock
- 1/4 cup (60 mL) chopped fresh flat-leaf parsley
- 1/4 cup (60 mL) butter, melted

- 1 tablespoon (15 mL) smoked paprika
- 12 oysters, shucked (page 135), liquor reserved
- Salt and freshly cracked black pepper

TURDUCKEN
- 1 turkey (25 lb/11.5 kg), boned
- 1/2 cup (125 mL) smoked paprika
- Salt and freshly cracked black pepper
- 1 duck (5 lb/2.25 kg), boned, wings discarded
- 1 chicken (3½ lb/1.6 kg), boned, wings discarded
- 1 fresh black truffle (optional)
- 1/2 cup (125 mL) butter, melted

GRAVY
- 2 tablespoons (30 mL) butter, softened
- 2 tablespoons (30 mL) all-purpose flour
- 2 cups (500 mL) veal or chicken stock
- 1/2 cup (125 mL) drippings from the turducken, fat skimmed off
- 2 tablespoons (30 mL) Dijon mustard
- Leaves from 3 sprigs of thyme
- Salt and freshly cracked black pepper

FOR THE CORN BREAD:
In the bowl of a stand mixer fitted with the dough hook, stir together the water, sugar, and salt. Sprinkle the yeast on top. Let sit for 5 minutes or until the mixture begins to

foam. Add the all-purpose flour and corn flour. Mix on low speed until well combined. Mix on medium speed until the dough is smooth and pulls away from the bowl, 4 to 5 minutes. (You can also knead the dough by hand until it is smooth and elastic.)

Remove the dough from the bowl, clean and dry the bowl, and oil it well with canola oil. Return the dough to the bowl, cover with plastic wrap, and let sit in a warm place for 2 hours or until doubled in size.

Line a baking sheet with parchment paper; dust the paper with flour. Turn the dough out onto a lightly floured work surface and punch it to push the air out. Shape it into a ball, then place it on the baking sheet. Slash the top of your loaf. Brush with the egg wash and sprinkle with flour and coarse salt. Let sit in a warm spot for 1 hour or until nearly doubled in size.

Preheat oven to 400°F (200°C).

Bake for 30 minutes or until the crust is golden brown and the loaf sounds hollow when the bottom is tapped. Cool completely on a rack.

FOR THE STUFFING:
Cut the corn bread into cubes; set aside.

In a large skillet, heat the oil over medium-high heat. Add the sausage;

cook until golden brown, about 5 minutes. Add the celery, onion, red pepper, and garlic; continue cooking until the onion is translucent, about 5 minutes. Deglaze with the stock. Stir in the cornbread. Transfer to a large bowl. Stir in the parsley, melted butter, paprika, and oysters with their liquor. Season with salt and pepper. Cover and refrigerate if not using immediately.

FOR THE TURDUCKEN:
Preheat oven to 325°F (160°C).

FOR THE TURKEY:
Spread the turkey skin side down on a work surface, turning the leg, thigh, and wing meat to the outside to expose as much meat as you can. Sprinkle the meat evenly with about 3 tablespoons (45 mL) of the smoked paprika, patting the seasoning in with your hands. Season with salt and pepper.

Measure 4 cups (1 L) of the stuffing. Stuff some of this stuffing into the leg, thigh, and wing cavities until full but not tightly packed. (If too tightly packed, the legs and wings may burst open during cooking.) Spread an even layer of the stuffing over the remaining exposed meat, 1/2 to 3/4 inch (1 to 2 cm) thick.

FOR THE DUCK:
Cut away and set aside some of the duck fat. (You can freeze the fat and use it for sautéing vegetables.) Place the duck, skin down, on top of the stuffing, arranging the duck evenly over the stuffing. Season the meat evenly with about 1 tablespoon (15 mL) of the smoked paprika, patting it in with your hands. Season with salt and pepper. Spread about 1 cup (250 mL) of the remaining stuffing evenly over the exposed duck meat, about 1/2 inch (1 cm) thick.

FOR THE CHICKEN:
Stuff the chicken with the remaining stuffing. Place a truffle (if using) in the centre.

Enlist someone's help to close the turducken. Fold the sides of the turkey together to close the bird. Have your helper hold the turkey closed. Using a trussing needle and cotton string, and beginning at the neck, sew the two sides together snugly but not too tightly, making stitches about 1 inch (2.5 cm) apart. Turn the turducken breast side up and sew closed any openings. Tie the legs together just below the ends.

With the assistance of your helper, carefully lift the turducken into a 15- × 11- × 2½-inch (38 × 28 × 6 cm) baking pan. (This pan size is ideal because the turducken will fit snugly and retain its shape while cooking.) Tuck in the wings. Place the pan in a slightly larger pan with sides at least 2½ inches (6 cm) high, to catch the overflow of drippings during cooking. Sprinkle the turducken with the remaining smoked paprika, patting it in with your hands. Brush with the melted butter.

Bake for 4 hours or until a meat thermometer inserted into the centre reads 165°F (75°C). Slide strong spatulas underneath the turducken (remember there are no bones to support the bird's structure) and carefully transfer it to a platter. Cover loosely with foil and let rest for about 15 minutes.

FOR THE GRAVY:
In a small bowl, make a beurre manié by mashing together the butter and flour.

In a medium saucepan, combine the stock, turducken drippings, mustard, thyme, and beurre manié. Season with salt and pepper. Bring the gravy to a boil, whisking to dissolve the beurre manié. Turn down heat to medium low and simmer, stirring occasionally, for 10 minutes.

Present the turducken to your guests before carving. Be sure to make your slices crosswise so that each slice contains the stuffing and all three meats. Serve with the gravy.

COOK'S NOTE:
You can assemble the turducken a day ahead. Cover and refrigerate until needed.

et de l'alimentation sur
étoffent notre char-
forment notre corps
d'un caractère net-
souvent difficile à
ais le savoir culi-
naître parfaite-
oit jouer une
intelligente,
rer l'orga-
ance à la

inée a
déve-
c'est
res
a-

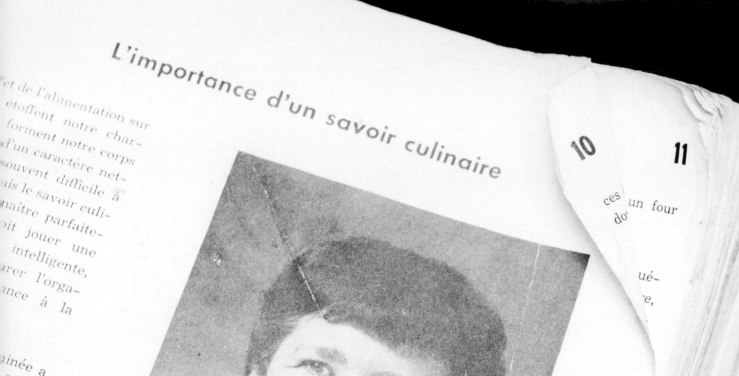

Mme Jehane Benoît

es règles fondamentales de   contré une cuisinière ayant un vaste
                                  répertoire de recettes et qui pourtant
encyclopédie de la cui-   commettait une faute aussi élémen-
, vous trouverez ces   taire que d'oublier de retirer les
ntales décrites dans   œufs brouillés du feu avant la fin de
tres — aliments de   la cuisson, puisque ceux-ci conti-
umes, pain, menus,   nuent à cuire quelques secondes
'il est inutile   même après avoir été retirés

J'espè

ces un four
do

é...re,

do.
pétis-
ières
du
aux

WOMEN IN THE KITCHEN

BISON TARTARE

SEAFOOD STEW WITH GARLIC ROUILLE CROUTONS

SEAFOOD STOCK

NO-KNEAD BREAD WITH ROASTED CINNAMON PLUMS AND HONEY BUTTER

Although the restaurant industry can be a bit of a boy's club, my cooking has been greatly influenced by learning from and cooking with women in the kitchen. My mom first taught me how to cook, and she was the one who pushed me to go further with my career, to dream bigger and aim higher. She taught me invaluable lessons even before I ever wanted to be a professional cook. When I was a kid, I was always my mom's sous-chef. She would say to me, "Charles, a chef works efficiently, a chef cleans his station, a chef does dishes." It's possible she just didn't want me making a big mess in her kitchen, but in the end, she was right.

Jehane Benoît is one of my culinary heroes. She was a Québécoise cookbook author, radio and television host, journalist, and food pioneer way ahead of her time. Quebec's version of Julia Child, she was a huge advocate of Québécois cuisine, and her book *L'Encyclopédie de la Cuisine* is one of the most influential cookbooks in my life. In 1925 she started an English/French cooking school in Montreal, and she helped define what we now know as distinct Québécois and Canadian cuisines. For all you vegetarians out there, she opened the Salad Bar, one of the first Canadian restaurants to focus on vegetarian cuisine, in the 1930s. Vegetarians and I don't always see eye to eye, but I think we can all agree, that's pretty cool.

I also have the utmost respect for Julia Child and Alice Waters, and I know you're going to think I'm crazy, but one of my favourite cookbooks of all time is Martha Stewart's *Entertaining*. It's total culinary madness! She's entertaining in a world where money is no object, and her displays of food are so over the top, they verge on fantasy. I want to live in that book!

When I think of women in the kitchen today, there are three chefs in particular I really admire. In Montreal, there's Emma. She worked at Globe with my mentors Dave and Fred and went on to work with them at Liverpool House. She's finally realized her dream of having her own place, Nora Gray, and it's one of Montreal's best restaurants. Her kitchen has a totally different vibe than mine. Emma is calm, cool, and collected, but when the pressure is on, she can hammer it out like a maniac. Her total dedication to cooking and her natural talent are something you don't come across very often.

I worked with Marie-Fleur way back in the day at Tapeo. We got along on so many levels, but our real bond was that we both came from the same French-Canadian background and grew up the same way, eating the same things. We were two French Quebecers working in a tapas restaurant, and although we were dedicated to that Spanish menu, we always tried to showcase a little bit of Quebec in our dishes. Since then, Marie-Fleur has become the big boss, and Tapeo is a real success story. She has a knack for simple flavour combinations that always make me go, "Why didn't I think of this?"

Last but certainly not least is Tracy. Her restaurant, the Belworth House, in Norfolk County, Ontario, doubles as a cooking school. Tracy's whole philosophy is farm to table, and she really loves food—her licence plate even reads "IMCOOKN." I first met Tracy when I started doing *Chuck's Day Off* and went to a food fair in Norfolk. Tracy was assigned to be my assistant. She'd never seen my show, so I think she was skeptical about my abilities. Once she saw me work, however, I knew I had gained her respect. We were making small talk and she just said, out of the blue, "Maybe you'll be on *Iron Chef* one day." I told her, "That's totally nuts, but if I am, you can come." Four years later when I was invited onto the show, she was the first person I told. I really admire Tracy because she believes that knowing where food comes from is just as important as knowing how to cook, so much so that when she's not cooking, she's teaching.

But cooking isn't about gender, it's about food. The rewards of cooking are truly personal, and if you can't see the beauty in it, it's not for you. At the end of the day, all you take home is a job well done. I am thankful for all the women who not only are making their mark in the industry but also are mentors and teachers. They make professional kitchens a better place for everyone.

BISON TARTARE

PREP 15 MIN × COOK 8 MIN × SERVES 4

Ask your favourite butcher for the best possible bison meat. The rest is easy. This recipe makes more pickled mushrooms than you'll need for the tartare—but I always say, when pickling, more is more!

PICKLED OYSTER MUSHROOMS

- 1/2 lb (225 g) oyster mushroom clusters, grilled
- 4 cups (1 L) white vinegar
- 2 cups (500 mL) sugar
- 2 tablespoons (30 mL) chili flakes
- 1 tablespoon (15 mL) black peppercorns
- Salt

BISON TARTARE

- 1½ lb (675 g) bison sirloin, diced
- 2 shallots, minced
- 1 tablespoon (15 mL) olive oil
- 1 tablespoon (15 mL) Dijon mustard
- 1 teaspoon (5 mL) capers, drained
- Salt and freshly cracked black pepper

FRIED SHALLOTS

- Canola oil for deep-frying
- 4 shallots, thinly sliced
- Salt and freshly cracked black pepper

HERBETTE SALAD

- 2 tablespoons (30 mL) chopped fresh parsley
- 2 tablespoons (30 mL) minced fresh sorrel
- 1 tablespoon (15 mL) minced fresh chives
- 1 teaspoon (5 mL) olive oil
- 1 teaspoon (5 mL) white balsamic vinegar
- Salt and freshly cracked black pepper

FOR THE PICKLED OYSTER MUSHROOMS:

Place the mushrooms in a medium nonaluminum bowl. In a large saucepan, combine the vinegar, sugar, chili flakes, peppercorns, and salt to taste. Bring to a boil, reduce heat, and simmer until the sugar is dissolved, about 5 minutes. Pour over the mushrooms. Let cool to room temperature.

FOR THE BISON TARTARE:

In a medium bowl, combine the bison, shallots, olive oil, mustard, and capers. Strain 1/2 cup (125 mL) of the pickled mushrooms; coarsely chop them and add to the tartare. Season with salt and pepper. Mix gently but thoroughly.

FOR THE FRIED SHALLOTS:

In a deep, heavy saucepan, heat about 1 inch (2.5 cm) of canola oil to 350°F (180°C). Deep-fry the shallots until golden brown. Drain on paper towels. Season with salt and pepper.

FOR THE HERBETTE SALAD:

In a small bowl, combine the parsley, sorrel, chives, olive oil, and vinegar; season with salt and pepper. Toss.

To serve, divide the bison tartare among chilled plates. Garnish with the herbette salad and fried shallots.

SEAFOOD STEW WITH GARLIC ROUILLE CROUTONS

PREP 30 MIN × COOK 30 MIN × SERVES 4 TO 6

If you're a fan of shellfish, this stew is for you. With clams, lobster, crab, rock shrimp, and mussels, it's a fantastic feast. Modify it to your taste, adding or leaving out anything you want.

- Seafood Stock (page 130)

LEEKS AND SHIITAKE MUSHROOMS

- 2 tablespoons (30 mL) olive oil
- 4 small leeks (white and pale green parts only), halved lengthwise
- 1/2 lb (225 g) shiitake mushrooms, stemmed
- 2 red bell peppers, roasted, peeled, seeded, and sliced
- Salt and freshly cracked black pepper
- 1 cup (250 mL) fresh green peas

ROUILLE CROUTONS

- 6 to 8 thick slices country bread
- 3 garlic cloves, minced
- 1 fresh red chili, seeded and minced
- 1 large egg yolk
- 1 cup (250 mL) + 2 tablespoons (30 mL) olive oil
- Salt and freshly cracked black pepper

SEAFOOD STEW

- 1/2 lb (225 g) clams, scrubbed
- 1/2 lb (225 g) mussels, scrubbed
- 1/2 lb (225 g) rock shrimp
- Meat from 2 lobsters

FOR SERVING

- Meat from 4 cooked crab legs
- Olive oil for drizzling
- 4 to 6 fresh sea scallops on the shell
- Chopped fresh chervil

FOR THE LEEKS AND SHIITAKE MUSHROOMS:

Heat the oil in a large skillet over medium heat. Add the leeks and sauté until golden brown, about 10 minutes. Add the mushrooms; sauté until browned, about 5 minutes more. Add the roasted peppers (along with any of their juices) and a ladle of seafood stock. Season with salt and pepper. Remove from heat and keep warm.

FOR THE ROUILLE CROUTONS:

Soak 2 slices of the bread in the seafood stock. Squeeze out the liquid and add the bread to a food processor; add the garlic, chili, and egg yolk. Process to blend. With the motor running, slowly add 1 cup (250 mL) of the olive oil until a smooth paste forms. Add a little of the seafood stock if the rouille starts to break. Season with salt and pepper.

Heat the remaining 2 tablespoons (30 mL) oil in a large skillet over medium-high heat. Add the remaining 4 to 6 slices of bread (1 for each serving) and toast on both sides. Set aside and keep warm.

FOR THE SEAFOOD STEW:

Bring the seafood stock to a simmer. Add the clams; cook until they start to open, about 8 minutes. Add the mussels; cook until they open, another 2 minutes. Add the shrimp and lobster meat; simmer for 2 minutes. Discard any unopened mussels or clams.

To serve, add the peas to the shiitake mixture to warm them up. Spread the rouille on the toasted bread. Divide the shiitake mixture among shallow bowls, top with the crabmeat, and ladle the seafood stew into the bowls. Drizzle with olive oil. Garnish with a live scallop on the shell and sprinkle with chervil. Serve the rouille croutons on the side.

SEAFOOD STOCK

PREP 1 HOUR × COOK 3 HOURS × MAKES 2½ TO 3 CUPS

If you love shellfish soups and stews, make this stock in quantity and freeze. It will keep for 3 months.

- 3 tablespoons (45 mL) olive oil
- 1 carrot, chopped
- 1 celery rib, chopped
- 1 fennel bulb, chopped
- 1 head of garlic, halved crosswise
- 1 leek (white and pale green parts only), chopped
- 1 onion, chopped
- 3 tablespoons (45 mL) ketchup
- 4 sprigs of rosemary
- 4 sprigs of thyme
- Shells of 4 cooked crab legs (reserve meat for the stew page 128)
- Shells of 2 cooked lobsters (reserve meat for the stew page 128)
- 1 tablespoon (15 mL) black peppercorns
- 1 tablespoon (15 mL) butter
- Salt and freshly cracked black pepper

Heat the oil in a stockpot over medium heat. Add the carrot, celery, fennel, garlic, leek, and onion; sauté for 5 minutes. Stir in the ketchup, rosemary, thyme, and crab and lobster shells. Add the peppercorns. Cover with cold water. Bring to a boil, then reduce heat and simmer, uncovered, for 2 hours.

Strain the stock into a large saucepan, discarding the solids. Simmer over medium heat until reduced by two-thirds, about 45 minutes. Stir in the butter and season with salt and pepper.

NO-KNEAD BREAD

WITH ROASTED CINNAMON PLUMS AND HONEY BUTTER

PREP 20 MIN PLUS 30 MIN FOR RISING × COOK 80 MIN × MAKES 1 LOAF

Not a baker? Neither am I, but this no-knead recipe is way easier than pie.

BREAD

- 1½ cups (375 mL) warm water
- 1½ teaspoons (7 mL) active dry yeast
- 1 tablespoon (15 mL) sugar
- 1 tablespoon (15 mL) olive oil
- 1 teaspoon (5 mL) white vinegar
- 1½ cups (375 mL) all-purpose flour
- 1½ cups (375 mL) whole wheat flour
- 1 teaspoon (5 mL) coarse salt
- A sprinkle of raw sugar or maple sugar

ROASTED CINNAMON PLUMS

- 6 to 8 ripe purple plums, halved and pitted
- 2 tablespoons (30 mL) brown sugar
- 1 teaspoon (5 mL) cinnamon
- Zest of 1 lemon
- Maldon sea salt

HONEY BUTTER

- 1 cup (250 mL) butter, softened
- 1/4 cup (60 mL) honey

FOR THE BREAD:

In a large bowl, combine the water, yeast, and sugar. Let sit until it foams, about 5 minutes. Stir in the olive oil and vinegar. Add the all-purpose flour, whole wheat flour, and salt. Stir until the dough comes together and is a little wet and spongy but not sticky. If the dough feels sticky, add a touch more whole wheat flour, a little at a time, until no longer sticky. Cover with a damp kitchen towel and let rise in a warm place until doubled in size, 30 to 40 minutes.

Preheat oven to 400°F (200°C). Butter a loaf pan and line with parchment paper.

Using a big spatula, spoon the dough into the loaf pan. With a knife, make 2 or 3 shallow diagonal slashes in the loaf. Sprinkle with raw sugar.

Bake for 50 minutes or until the bread is golden brown and crusty on top and sounds hollow when tapped on the underside. Let sit (if you can wait!) for 5 to 10 minutes before turning out of the pan. Keep warm under a kitchen towel until ready to serve.

FOR THE ROASTED CINNAMON PLUMS:

Lower oven temperature to 350°F (180°C).

Place plums cut side up in a baking dish just large enough to hold them in one layer. Sprinkle with sugar, cinnamon, and lemon zest. Roast for 30 minutes or until soft. Sprinkle with Maldon salt.

FOR THE HONEY BUTTER:

While the plums are roasting, in a bowl cream together the butter and honey.

To serve, spread the honey butter on slices of warm bread. Spoon the plums over the bread.

COOK'S NOTE:

For a savoury version of this bread, sprinkle steak spice on the bread before baking instead of raw sugar.

THE OYSTER SHUCKERS

Fried Oyster Roll with Dynamite Sauce and Waffle Fries

Raw Oysters with Mignonnettes

Caesar Salad with Oyster Croutons

Maple Tapioca

Our oyster bar is a huge part of what makes Garde Manger special. In Mark Kurlansky's book *The Big Oyster: History on the Half Shell*, all about the history of the oyster in New York City, I read that back in the 1800s, oyster bars were marked by a red muslin balloon lit by a candle. They also happened to be rendezvous points where women of the night could meet prospective clients, similar to the brothels that were also marked by red lights. So oyster bars had a dual purpose: they were a place where anyone could enjoy oysters as big as steaks, and they also served to facilitate another enjoyable activity!

I thought it was cool that red lights distinguished oyster bars, so when we opened Garde Manger, we put one up above our front door. It actually ends up looking kind of pink, but you get the idea. At our other restaurant, Le Bremner, there is also a red light outside. It's a little piece of history that we thought was worth preserving.

My mom was the one who first taught me how to shuck an oyster. With all our big family gatherings and the fact that we are all obsessed with oysters, shucking was a skill that had been passed down through generations. Shucking became second nature for me—even though my mom and I now disagree about the right way to do it.

At a famous Montreal restaurant called Magnan's, there used to be an all-you-can-eat shuck-it-yourself oyster bar. My mom was pretty proud of her teenage son's shucking skills and would send me over to all the tables to help out people who were having trouble. You can imagine how mortified I was as my mom offered my services to the entire restaurant, but it did make me a better, faster shucker.

Not everyone can shuck an oyster. It's a real skill. It's about being able to read each oyster and open it properly, cleanly, and neatly—simplicity at its finest. You want to open the shell in a swift movement and not tear or stab the meat. It's a delicate operation, and if you're going to shuck at Garde Manger, you have to be incredibly fast because we sell a lot of oysters!

Shucking is more than just a connection with my family history. For me it's also about performing the act itself. I don't have to think, and I let my hands guide me. It's almost religious, this repetitive, fluid motion that comes so naturally. I can bring cases of oysters anywhere—parties, barbecues, special events—and all I need is a knife. Oysters always create something of a buzz. Whether they love them or hate them, everyone has an oyster story.

Don't get me wrong. When it comes to eating oysters, I'm not all romantic about it. I don't sit down to eat three and ponder life. I'll slurp back three dozen in one shot. That might be over the top, but I can't help myself.

My favourite oysters are from the East Coast: I think they kill any other oyster out there. The West Coast's are great too, but they've got nothing on oysters from New Brunswick, Nova Scotia, PEI, Massachusetts, and Maine. The East's are a bit more briny and salty—they really carry that plucked-from-the-ocean flavour—whereas West Coast oysters are milkier and not as salty, and have a mild, almost cucumber taste. It's all personal preference, so try them all to discover what you like.

One of my partners, Tim, has become our master shucker. Although he loved eating them, he had never really shucked before. Because I was so busy with the kitchen, Tim decided to step up to the oyster bar, and once he did, he never looked back. He's become so enthralled with the shucking world, he's even making a documentary about it.

In Montreal, we're lucky to have a growing community of oyster shuckers who are truly passionate about their craft and well respected for their work.

It's really incredible how far this little sea gem has come, and so this meal is for all the oyster shuckers and lovers out there.

HOW I SHUCK AN OYSTER

STEP 1: Get a cloth and a good oyster knife. Wrap your hand in the cloth to hold the oyster and also protect your hand.

STEP 2: Hold the oyster dome side down. The oyster has a bit of a teardrop shape. Insert the knife at the top of the teardrop, into the hinge.

STEP 3: Angle the knife downward, twist the knife to pop the hinge, and in one clean, fluid motion slide the knife in between the top shell and the oyster itself to sever the membrane that holds the oyster in place.

STEP 4: Remove the top shell. Sweep the knife along the bottom shell to release the oyster. Clean off any little bits that may have crumbled onto the oyster. Make sure the oyster is loose.

STEP 5: Slurp back and repeat!

FRIED OYSTER ROLL
WITH DYNAMITE SAUCE AND WAFFLE FRIES

PREP 30 MIN × COOK 15 MIN × SERVES 4 TO 6

I'll never say a bad thing about lobster rolls, but I'll say this: fried oyster rolls are like that new kid in school who knew all the yo-yo tricks.

DYNAMITE SAUCE
- 1/2 cup (125 mL) mayonnaise
- 2 tablespoons (30 mL) Sriracha hot sauce
- Salt and freshly cracked black pepper

OYSTERS
- 1/2 cup (125 mL) milk
- Juice of 1 lemon
- 1 garlic clove, smashed
- Salt and freshly cracked black pepper
- 18 to 24 oysters, shucked (page 135) and drained

TEMPURA BATTER
- 1½ cups (375 mL) all-purpose flour
- 1 tablespoon (15 mL) cornstarch
- 1½ cups (375 mL) sparkling water
- Salt and freshly cracked black pepper
- Cayenne pepper

WAFFLE FRIES
- Canola oil for deep-frying
- 4 Yukon Gold potatoes, unpeeled
- Smoked salt and freshly cracked black pepper

FOR SERVING
- Chopped iceberg lettuce
- 6 hot dog buns, buttered and grilled
- Tobiko
- Bonito flakes

FOR THE DYNAMITE SAUCE:
In a small bowl, stir together the mayonnaise and Sriracha. Season with salt and pepper. Refrigerate until ready to serve.

FOR THE OYSTERS:
In a small bowl, combine the milk, lemon juice, and garlic. Season with salt and pepper. Add the oysters. Set aside for about 15 minutes.

FOR THE TEMPURA BATTER:
While the oysters marinate, in a medium bowl, whisk together 1 cup (250 mL) of the flour and the cornstarch. Add the sparkling water and whisk again until the batter is smooth. Season with salt and pepper.

In a shallow bowl, combine the remaining 1/2 cup (125 mL) flour and the cayenne. Set aside.

FOR THE WAFFLE FRIES:
In a deep-fryer or deep, heavy sauce-pan, heat 2 inches (5 cm) of canola oil to 350°F (180°C).

Using a vegetable slicer with a ripple blade, cut a 1/8-inch (3 mm) crosswise slice from a potato. Rotate the potato one-quarter turn and make the next cut. Continue to rotate the potato a quarter turn back and forth for each cut to give the slices a basket-weave design.

Working in batches, deep-fry for 2 minutes or until golden brown. Drain on paper towels. Season with smoked salt and pepper.

TO FRY THE OYSTERS:
Heat the canola oil to 375°F (190°C).

Drain the oysters. Working in batches, dredge them in the seasoned flour, then dip them in the tempura batter. Gently place them in the hot oil. Fry for 1 minute or until they are deep golden in colour. Drain on paper towels. Season with salt and pepper.

To serve, spoon chopped lettuce inside hot dog buns. Nestle 3 or 4 fried oysters in the lettuce; drizzle with dynamite sauce. Garnish with tobiko and bonito flakes.

RAW OYSTERS WITH MIGNONNETTES

PREP 15 MIN × SERVES 4

In my opinion, raw is the best way to enjoy an oyster. It's simple, perfect, and totally addictive.

- 24 oysters, such as Malpeque, Kumamoto, or Belon
- Crushed ice or seaweed
- Mignonnettes (page 202)

Scrub the oysters under cold water with a stiff brush to remove the dirt, especially in the hinge area where mud has a tendency to get trapped.

Shuck the oysters according to the instructions on page 135. Serve on the half shell in a bed of crushed ice or seaweed to keep them steady. Spoon your choice of mignonnette over the oysters.

CAESAR SALAD WITH OYSTER CROUTONS

PREP 15 MIN × COOK 10 MIN × SERVES 4

This Caesar salad is one of my favourites. Whether you include the oyster croutons or not, this salad is going to become a staple.

CAESAR SALAD

- 3 slices bacon, diced
- 1 garlic clove, smashed
- 2 or 3 anchovies, to taste
- 2 tablespoons (30 mL) Dijon mustard
- 1 large egg yolk
- 1/2 cup (125 mL) vegetable oil
- Juice of 1 lemon
- 1 cup (125 mL) grated Parmigiano-Reggiano cheese
- Freshly cracked black pepper
- 2 romaine hearts, leaves separated

OYSTER CROUTONS

- Canola oil for deep-frying
- 12 oysters, shucked (page 135)
- Flour for dredging

FOR THE CAESAR SALAD:

Cook the bacon until crispy. Drain on paper towels. Set aside.

Using a mortar and pestle, mash the garlic, anchovies, and mustard to a paste. Add the egg yolk; mash until blended. Whisking constantly, drizzle in the vegetable oil until the dressing emulsifies. Whisk in the lemon juice and half of the Parmesan. Season with pepper.

FOR THE OYSTER CROUTONS:

In a deep-fryer or deep, heavy saucepan, heat 2 inches (5 cm) of canola oil to 350°F (180°C).

Dredge the oysters in the flour. Fry for 2 minutes or until golden brown. Drain on paper towels.

To serve, in a salad bowl, toss the romaine lettuce with the dressing. Add the bacon and remaining Parmesan. Season with freshly cracked black pepper. Garnish with the oyster croutons.

MAPLE TAPIOCA

PREP 10 MIN × COOK 45 MIN × SERVES 6

I bake this creamy tapioca in the oven, then finish it like a crème brûlée, giving it a glassy, crunchy layer of caramelized maple sugar.

- 3 cups (750 mL) milk
- 1 cup (250) whipping cream
- Peel of 1 orange
- 1 vanilla bean
- 1/2 cup (125 mL) pearl tapioca (not instant)
- 4 large egg yolks
- 1/2 cup (125 mL) maple syrup
- A pinch of salt
- 1/4 cup (60 mL) maple sugar

Preheat oven to 300°F (150°C).

In a medium saucepan, combine the milk, cream, and orange peel. Scrape the seeds from the vanilla bean into the cream, then add the pod. Bring to a simmer. Stir in the tapioca.

In a large bowl, whisk together the egg yolks, maple syrup, and salt. Whisking constantly, pour in one-third of the tapioca mixture. Whisk the yolk mixture back into the pot of tapioca. Simmer over medium-low heat, stirring constantly with a heatproof spatula, until thick enough to coat the back of a spoon, about 5 minutes. Discard the orange peel and vanilla pod.

Divide the pudding among six 6-oz (175 mL) ramekins; transfer to a baking sheet. Bake, uncovered, until the puddings are firm around the edges and jiggly in the centre, about 30 minutes. Sprinkle maple sugar evenly over each pudding. Broil until the top is bubbling and golden, 3 to 5 minutes. Watch carefully to make sure it doesn't burn. Serve warm or cold.

THE FLOOR STAFF

SEARED TROUT WITH FENNEL SALAD
VEGETARIAN SHEPHERD'S PIE
GOAT CHEESE MASHED POTATOES
HOMEMADE KETCHUP
LEMON POUND CAKE WITH PISTACHIO CREAM AND STRAWBERRIES

From the time customers walk in the door to the moment they step out, it's the floor staff's job to take care of them. It requires a special combination of professionalism and personality, whether you're a busboy or a server, a hostess or the manager. The floor staff need to be involved in everything—they need to know what's going on in the kitchen, they need to know the menu, the ingredients, the wines, the cocktails, the oysters—everything. They need to be on top of their game at all times. They're the face of a restaurant, and having a good floor staff can make or break a dining experience.

As much as people come to tell us how great that evening's food was, even more of them tell us how impressed they were with the amazing and professional service. Every time I walk into the restaurant and see all my floor staff smiling and busy, working hard and having a good time, I realize that they care as much about this place as my partners and I do. The most important thing for us is to let the staff get involved and educate them as much as we can. Just as with cooks, it's all about taste, taste, taste. Letting the floor staff taste everything helps them understand it and sell it.

The menu at Garde Manger changes all the time, so the floor staff need to know exactly what's in every dish so they can explain it to the customers. People have food allergies, people don't like certain ingredients, or they've never heard of an ingredient, so it's extremely important that my staff know every single detail, right down to the garnish.

The floor staff at Garde Manger are a big part of the restaurant's success. Without their commitment and energy, we wouldn't even be close to what we are today. Two of the staff who go that extra mile to make the place their own are Jess and Pat.

Jess joined us about two months after we opened, and she's become an invaluable part of the restaurant. This place is just as much hers as it is mine. Jess started as a bartender and slowly moved her way up to assistant manager, then manager, and today she's our general manager, taking care of the day-to-day business that keeps our restaurant afloat. To be able to do what she does, she needs to be a teacher, a psychologist, an accountant, and a friend. As much as this job has changed her life, it has also changed mine. She's more than just an essential part of the team—she makes the team.

Then there's Pat. Pat is our night manager, and he's a total maniac! I've known him for at least ten years, and although he's been at the restaurant only for a short while, what a difference he's made. Pat takes "lean, mean machine" to the next level. He's really into running, to the point where no matter what time of year, whether it's forty below or humid as hell, he runs to and from work every day—and that doesn't include the 25 kilometres he runs *during* the day. It's insane, but I love it! As a manager, Pat is very demanding and plays a huge part in making sure nothing slips up. He holds everyone and everything to a higher standard, and that's what makes him so valuable.

In a restaurant, no matter how much planning you do, no matter your expertise, it's never going to be perfect. You might come close, but it's this constant drive for perfection that counts. Jess and Pat always try to make today better than yesterday, all the while learning how to improve tomorrow. They really are our fearless leaders.

SEARED TROUT WITH FENNEL SALAD

PREP 15 MIN × COOK 2 MIN × SERVES 4

This has to be one of the most popular recipes from the show. It's the toasted spice mix that adds so much personality as well as a little crunch to the seared fish.

SHAVED FENNEL SALAD

- 1 fennel bulb, thinly sliced lengthwise
- 2 celery ribs, thinly sliced
- Celery leaves, chopped
- Leaves from a few sprigs of parsley, finely chopped
- Juice of 1/2 lemon
- 3 tablespoons (45 mL) olive oil
- Maldon sea salt and freshly cracked black pepper

TROUT

- 1 teaspoon (5 mL) fennel seeds, crushed
- 1 teaspoon (5 mL) mustard seeds, crushed
- 1 teaspoon (5 mL) dill seeds, crushed
- 1 teaspoon (5 mL) black peppercorns, crushed
- 1 teaspoon (5 mL) sea salt
- 1 tablespoon (15 mL) olive oil
- 4 skin-on trout fillets (4 oz/115 g each)
- 2 tablespoons (30 mL) vegetable oil

FOR THE FENNEL SALAD:

In a large bowl, combine the fennel, celery, celery leaves, parsley, lemon juice, and olive oil. Toss. Season with Maldon salt and pepper. Set aside.

FOR THE TROUT:

In a medium bowl, mix all the spices with the olive oil. Add the trout and turn to coat each piece with the spice mixture.

Heat the vegetable oil in a large skillet over medium-high heat. Sear the trout skin side down for 1 minute or until crispy. Flip and cook on the other side for 30 seconds or longer if you prefer it well-done.

To serve, divide the trout among 4 plates. Garnish with the shaved fennel salad.

VEGETARIAN SHEPHERD'S PIE

PREP 30 MIN × COOK 2 HOURS × SERVES 8 TO 10

I love this meatless take on a comfort classic. It freezes really well, so having leftovers is never a problem.

SPAGHETTI SQUASH
- 1 spaghetti squash (about 3 lb/1.35 kg)
- Salt and freshly cracked black pepper

ROASTED GARLIC
- 1 head of garlic, top sliced off to expose the cloves
- 1 tablespoon (15 mL) olive oil
- Salt and freshly cracked black pepper

BREAD CRUMBS
- 2 cups (500 mL) fresh bread crumbs
- 1 cup (250 mL) milk
- 1/4 cup (60 mL) pine nuts, toasted
- 1 tablespoon (15 mL) chopped fresh basil
- 1 tablespoon (15 mL) chopped fresh thyme
- 1 tablespoon (15 mL) chopped fresh flat-leaf parsley
- 2 eggs, beaten
- Salt and freshly cracked black pepper

VEGETABLE MIXTURE
- 1 cup (250 mL) du Puy lentils
- 2 tablespoons (30 mL) olive oil
- 2 carrots, finely chopped
- 2 celery ribs, finely chopped
- 1 onion, chopped
- 4 garlic cloves, minced
- 1 lb (450 g) mixed mushrooms, stemmed and coarsely chopped
- 1/2 lb (225 g) mixed mushrooms, stemmed and sliced
- Salt and freshly cracked black pepper
- Goat Cheese Mashed Potatoes (page 152)

GARNISH
- Fried shallots

FOR THE SPAGHETTI SQUASH:
Preheat oven to 300°F (150°C).

Cut the squash in half lengthwise and remove the seeds. Place cut side down on a lightly oiled baking sheet and bake for 1½ hours or until the flesh is tender when pierced with a knife. (Alternatively, place cut side up on a microwave-safe plate and microwave at High for about 20 minutes, flipping it halfway through.) Using a fork, gently scrape strands into a bowl. Season and set aside.

FOR THE ROASTED GARLIC:
While the squash is baking, put the garlic on a square of foil. Drizzle with the olive oil and season. Tightly seal the garlic. Bake for 30 minutes or until very tender and caramelized. Unwrap and set aside.

FOR THE BREAD CRUMBS:
Meanwhile, in a medium bowl, combine the bread crumbs and milk; let stand for 5 minutes, until all the milk has been absorbed. Stir in the pine nuts, basil, thyme, parsley, and eggs. Season and set aside.

FOR THE VEGETABLE MIXTURE:
In a medium saucepan, combine the lentils, 4 cups (1 L) water, and a pinch of salt. Simmer, stirring occasionally, until the lentils are just tender, 15 to 20 minutes. Drain well.

Heat the oil in a large skillet over medium-high heat. Add the carrots, celery, and onion; cook, stirring frequently, until the onions are soft and translucent, about 5 minutes. Add the garlic and mushrooms; continue cooking until the vegetables are brown, about 10 minutes. Remove from heat. Stir in the lentils and bread crumb mixture. Season with salt and pepper.

TO ASSEMBLE:
Preheat oven to 450°F (230°C).

Spoon the vegetable mixture into an 11- × 9-inch (2.5 L) baking dish. Spread the spaghetti squash evenly over top. Spoon the potatoes over the squash, smoothing the top. Bake, uncovered, for 30 minutes or until the top is slightly browned. Garnish with fried shallots. Serve with Homemade Ketchup (page 152).

COOK'S NOTE:
This shepherd's pie freezes well, but if you don't want to make a large pie, the recipe is easily divided by half.

GOAT CHEESE MASHED POTATOES

PREP 15 MIN × COOK 20 MIN × SERVES 6

- 5 to 6 Yukon Gold potatoes, unpeeled
- 1 cup (250 mL) whipping cream
- 1/2 cup (125 mL) soft goat cheese
- 1/4 cup (60 mL) butter, melted
- Roasted garlic (page 150)
- Salt and freshly cracked black pepper

Cut the potatoes in half or thirds. Cook, covered, in a pot of boiling salted water until tender, 15 to 20 minutes. Drain well and return to the pot. Mash the potatoes; add the cream, goat cheese, melted butter, and roasted garlic; mash or stir until smooth. Season with salt and pepper. Set aside.

HOMEMADE KETCHUP

PREP 30 MIN × COOK 1 HOUR × MAKES 4 CUPS (1 L)

My grandmother used to make this for me when I was a kid, usually to go with her tourtière. My version can be used on practically anything, but it's especially good on my vegetarian shepherd's pie.

- 2 tablespoons (30 mL) olive oil
- 1 onion, diced
- 1 garlic clove, minced
- 2 Granny Smith apples, peeled and diced
- 1 peach, peeled and diced
- 6 to 8 tomatoes, peeled and coarsely chopped
- 1/2 cup (125 mL) brown sugar
- 1/2 cup (125 mL) cider vinegar
- 1/2 teaspoon (2 mL) chili flakes
- Dash of garlic hot pepper sauce
- 1 cinnamon stick
- 3 whole cloves
- Salt and freshly cracked black pepper

In a large saucepan over medium-high heat, combine the oil, onion, garlic, apples, and peach; sauté until the onion is translucent, about 5 minutes. Add the tomatoes, brown sugar, vinegar, chili flakes, hot pepper sauce, cinnamon stick, and cloves. Season with salt and pepper. Reduce heat and simmer gently, uncovered, for about 1 hour, until reduced by half. Discard the cinnamon stick and cloves. (*Ketchup keeps, covered and refrigerated, for 1 week.*)

LEMON POUND CAKE *WITH* PISTACHIO CREAM AND STRAWBERRIES

PREP 30 MIN × COOK 45 MIN × SERVES 8 TO 10

Lemon, strawberries, and cream can do no wrong together. For this recipe, the proof is definitely on the plate.

LEMON POUND CAKE

- 4 large eggs, separated
- 1 cup (250 mL) sugar
- 1 tablespoon (15 mL) vanilla extract
- Zest and juice of 1 lemon, plus additional zest for garnish
- 1 cup (250 mL) butter, melted and cooled to room temperature
- 1¾ cups (425 mL) all-purpose flour

PISTACHIO CREAM

- 1 cup (250 mL) crème fraîche
- 3 tablespoons (45 mL) brown sugar
- 1/4 cup (60 mL) pistachios, toasted and coarsely chopped

STRAWBERRIES

- 3 cups (750 mL) strawberries, halved
- 1/4 cup (60 mL) sugar
- Seeds scraped from 1 vanilla bean

FOR THE LEMON POUND CAKE:

Preheat oven to 400°F (200°C). Butter an 8- × 4-inch (1.5 L) loaf pan and line with parchment paper.

In a large bowl with an electric mixer, beat the egg whites until firm peaks form. Set aside.

In another large bowl, beat the egg yolks with the sugar, vanilla, and lemon zest until pale and creamy. Beat in the melted butter, then the lemon juice. Add the flour and stir until just combined. Gently but thoroughly fold in the egg whites.

Pour the batter into the loaf pan. Bake for 45 to 50 minutes or until a toothpick inserted in the centre comes out clean. Cool completely in the pan.

FOR THE PISTACHIO CREAM:

In a large bowl with an electric mixer, beat the crème fraîche with the brown sugar until thick. Stir in the pistachios. Refrigerate until ready to serve.

FOR THE STRAWBERRIES:

In a bowl, combine the strawberries, sugar, and vanilla seeds. Stir well. Let sit for about 30 minutes to allow the sugar to dissolve.

To serve, top slices of the pound cake with strawberries and then the pistachio cream. Garnish with lemon zest.

COOK'S NOTES:

In French, pound cake is called *quatre quarts*, or four quarters, because it consists of four main ingredients of equal weight: eggs, sugar, butter, and flour. You can leave out the lemon and change the flavour. Use almond extract to make it an almond pound cake. Add a shot of espresso to make it a coffee pound cake. Replace 1/4 cup (60 mL) of the flour with good-quality cocoa powder to make a chocolate pound cake.

For a different twist, butter the slices of cake, sprinkle with a mix of cinnamon and sugar, and grill them before topping with the strawberries and pistachio cream.

THE
BARTENDERS

PICKLED CLAM CAESAR

PRETZELS WITH CHEESY SAUCE

TURKEY WINGS WITH BLUE CHEESE DIP

PORK CRACKLING WITH COLESLAW, TROUT RILLETTES, AND SPICY RAPINI DIP

I used to be a bartender back when I was younger, and it was one of my favourite jobs. There's something about having control of that space, with a long bar separating you from the rest of the room, that's truly empowering. People always watch the bar. It's the epicentre of action, drink making, and banter that draws the clientele in and keeps them wanting to stay for more.

When I eat out I love to sit at the bar. It's a lively spot where a lot of the action happens, and it gives a real sense of the place. From the moment we decided to open Garde Manger, we knew we wanted to have seats at the bar for dining.

Bartending at Garde Manger is not just about making vodka sodas. It's actually one of the most challenging jobs at the restaurant. Not only do bartenders need to know their cocktails but they also have to fill the floor staff's orders for wine, mixed drinks, water, and coffee, all the while serving the customers sitting along the bar. There's a lot going on at once, and bartenders need to have a good head on their shoulders to manage it all.

At Garde Manger we have a bar licence, so if you wanted to you could just come in for the booze. After the kitchen closes at midnight, the straight-up bar crowd comes in, and the party goes on until closing time (in Montreal, that means 3 a.m.). The bartenders not only have to do a whole dinner service, they then need to hustle to attend to the rowdier drinking crowd.

We pride ourselves on making great cocktails, and we have a new drink every night. The weather, the season, what's fresh, and what we have on hand inspire us—anything goes and there are no rules. These

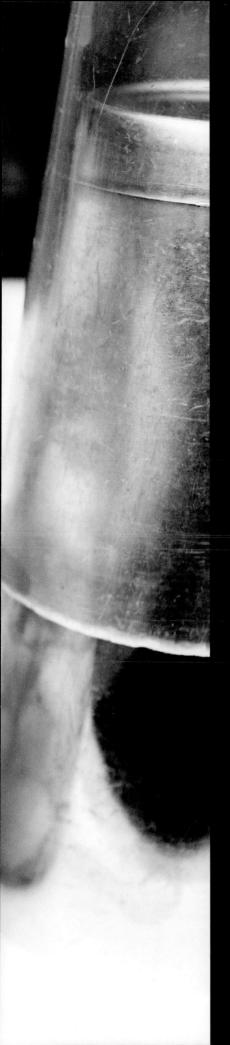

drinks are a bit more complicated than your average mix, and the bartenders need to be able to whip them up two, three, four at a time. They've got to be fast, and it's a tight space, so they also have to be coordinated. It's a real workout!

There is no textbook for being a good bartender—you either have it or you don't. All of Garde Manger's incredible bartenders have it in spades. Zoe in particular has made our bar a great place to be. She helped build this place, literally and figuratively. She's been here since day one and her hard work has defined what customers can expect from all our bartenders: the best.

PICKLED CLAM CAESAR

PREP 5 MIN PLUS OVERNIGHT FOR PICKLING × COOK 25 MIN × SERVES 4

The national cocktail of Canada is the Bloody Caesar, which we make with Clamato, a mixture of tomato and clam juices. As usual, I like to take it over the top by adding my own pickled clams to this patriotic mix.

PICKLED CLAMS
- 2 celery ribs, cut in chunks
- 1 cup (250 mL) water
- 8 medium clams, scrubbed
- 2 tablespoons (30 mL) soy sauce
- 2 tablespoons (30 mL) red wine vinegar
- 1 tablespoon (15 mL) sugar
- 1 teaspoon (5 mL) Worcestershire sauce
- Salt and freshly cracked black pepper

TOMATO JUICE
- 1 can (28 oz/796 mL) plum tomatoes
- Salt and freshly cracked black pepper

GARNISHES
- 3 tablespoons (45 mL) grated fresh horseradish
- 1 fresh chili pepper, minced
- Zest of 1 lemon
- Vodka, to taste
- Salt and freshly cracked black pepper

FOR THE PICKLED CLAMS:

Purée the celery in a blender, adding a little water if necessary. Set aside.

In a medium saucepan, bring the water to a simmer. Add the clams, cover, and cook for about 8 minutes, until they start to open. Using a slotted spoon, transfer the clams to a small bowl.

Add the soy sauce, vinegar, sugar, Worcestershire sauce, and puréed celery to the clam cooking water. Season with salt and pepper. Simmer for about 15 minutes, until reduced and thick. Strain over the clams. Cover and refrigerate overnight.

FOR THE TOMATO JUICE:

In a blender, purée the tomatoes. Strain, then season with salt and pepper.

To serve, put a few ice cubes in 4 tall glasses. Pour in some of the clam pickling liquid. Add some grated horseradish, chili pepper, and lemon zest. Add vodka (or omit if you are making a non-alcoholic drink). Top up with tomato juice and garnish with pickled clams. Season with salt and pepper.

PRETZELS WITH CHEESY SAUCE

PREP 45 MIN PLUS 2 HOURS FOR RISING × COOK 15 MIN × MAKES 6 LARGE PRETZELS

These pretzels remind me of going to watch baseball games when I was a kid. Don't worry about trying to make them look perfect. Once they're dipped in cheese, it doesn't matter what shape they are.

PRETZELS

- 1½ cups (375 mL) warm water (110 to 115°F/43 to 46°C)
- 1 tablespoon (15 mL) sugar
- 2 teaspoons (10 mL) active dry yeast
- 2 teaspoons (10 mL) kosher salt
- 3 cups (750 mL) all-purpose flour
- 2 tablespoons (30 mL) butter, melted
- 10 cups (2.5 L) cold water
- 2/3 cup (150 mL) baking soda
- Egg wash (1 egg yolk beaten with 1 tablespoon/15 mL water)
- Coarse salt

CHEESY SAUCE

- 1/2 cup (125 mL) beer
- 1 cup (250 mL) shredded sharp orange Cheddar cheese (4 oz/115 g)
- 1 tablespoon (15 mL) all-purpose flour
- 1 cup (250 mL) cream cheese, cubed and softened
- 1 garlic clove, minced
- 1 jalapeño pepper, minced
- Salt and freshly cracked black pepper

FOR THE PRETZELS:

Combine the warm water, sugar, yeast, and salt in the bowl of a stand mixer fitted with the dough hook. Let sit for 5 minutes or until the mixture begins to foam. Add the flour and melted butter; mix on low speed until well combined. Knead on medium speed until the dough is smooth and pulls away from the bowl, 4 to 5 minutes. (You can also knead the dough by hand until it is smooth and elastic.)

Remove the dough from the bowl, clean and dry the bowl, and oil it well with canola oil. Return the dough to the bowl, cover with plastic wrap, and let sit in a warm place until doubled in size, about 1 hour.

Line a baking sheet with parchment paper and brush with canola oil.

Turn the dough out onto a lightly oiled work surface and divide it into 6 equal pieces. Working with one piece of dough at a time, roll into a 24-inch (60 cm) rope. Make a U-shape with the rope. Cross the ends of the rope over each other and gently press them onto the bottom of the U to form the shape of a pretzel. Transfer the pretzel to the baking sheet. Continue with the remaining dough. Refrigerate the pretzels, uncovered, for 1 hour.

Preheat oven to 450°F (230°C).

Bring the cold water and baking soda to a boil in a large pot or roasting pan. Working with one or two pretzels at a time, boil pretzels for 30 seconds. (This will create the brown crunchy pretzel crust.) Remove them from the water using a large slotted spoon or flat spatula and arrange the pretzels on the baking sheet. Brush the tops with the egg wash and sprinkle with coarse salt. Bake until dark golden brown, 12 to 14 minutes. Cool on a rack for at least 5 minutes before serving.

FOR CHEESY SAUCE:

In a medium saucepan over medium heat, bring the beer to a simmer. In a bowl, stir together the Cheddar cheese and flour. Add the cream cheese, garlic, jalapeño, and Cheddar mixture to the beer; stir until all the cheese has melted and the sauce is smooth, about 5 minutes. Season with salt and black pepper.

Serve the pretzels with the cheesy sauce for dipping.

COOK'S NOTES:

Partially cooking the pretzels in boiling soda water gives them their characteristic shiny brown crunchy crust. Baking soda will not give the exact same brown, shiny crust as the traditional lye bath, but it's very close and much safer to use at home. For a different taste, instead of a salty topping, sprinkle with sesame seeds, poppy seeds, Parmesan, or cinnamon sugar.

TURKEY WINGS WITH BLUE CHEESE DIP

PREP 30 MIN PLUS 8 HOURS FOR BRINING × COOK 1½ HOURS × SERVES 8

Bigger, meatier, and a nice change from your puny everyday chicken wings, these spicy turkey wings will perk up any party.

BRINE AND WINGS
- 4 cups (1 L) water
- 1/2 cup (125 mL) kosher salt
- 1/2 cup (125 mL) brown sugar
- 1 onion, quartered
- 1 head of garlic, halved crosswise
- A bunch of parsley
- Juice of 2 oranges
- Juice of 2 lemons
- 1 tablespoon (15 mL) black peppercorns
- 1 tablespoon (15 mL) chili flakes
- 5 lb (2.25 kg) turkey wings (about 10 wings)
- Canola oil for frying

HOT PEPPER SAUCE
- 1/4 cup (60 mL) red hot pepper sauce (such as Sriracha)
- 3 tablespoons (45 mL) butter
- 2 tablespoons (30 mL) white wine vinegar
- Zest and juice of 1 lemon

SEASONED FLOUR
- 1 cup (250 mL) all-purpose flour
- 2 tablespoons (30 mL) smoked paprika
- 1 teaspoon (5 mL) cayenne pepper
- 1 teaspoon (5 mL) salt

BLUE CHEESE DIP
- 1/2 cup (125 mL) crumbled blue cheese
- 1/4 cup (60 mL) sour cream
- 1 tablespoon (15 mL) finely chopped fresh chives
- Juice of 1 lemon
- Salt and freshly cracked black pepper

FOR THE BRINE AND WINGS:
In a large saucepan, bring the water to a boil. Stir in the kosher salt and brown sugar. Cook until the salt and sugar are dissolved, about 2 minutes. Remove from heat and add the onion, garlic, parsley, orange juice, lemon juice, peppercorns, and chili flakes. Let cool. (You can add some ice to cool the brine a little faster.)

Add the wings to the brine. Top up with cold water if necessary to cover the wings. Cover and refrigerate for at least 8 hours and up to 12 hours.

Drain the wings, discarding the brine. Pat wings dry with paper towels. Cut off the wing tips (reserve them for turkey stock or soups). Cut the wings in half at the joint.

FOR THE HOT PEPPER SAUCE:
In a small saucepan, combine the hot pepper sauce, butter, vinegar, and lemon zest and juice. Cook over medium heat, stirring occasionally, until the butter is melted. Remove from heat.

FOR THE SEASONED FLOUR:
In a medium bowl, whisk together the flour, paprika, cayenne, and salt.

TO COOK THE WINGS:
Preheat oven to 350°F (180°C). Line a baking sheet with parchment paper.

In a deep-fryer or deep, heavy saucepan, heat about 3 inches (8 cm) of canola oil over medium-high heat. Dredge the wings in the seasoned flour, shaking off excess. Working in batches, fry the wings in a single layer, without crowding the pan, for 10 minutes, turning once, until browned. Drain on paper towels.

Arrange the wings on the baking sheet. Brush with some of the hot pepper sauce. Bake for 1½ hours, turning once and basting occasionally with sauce, until the wings are fork-tender.

FOR THE BLUE CHEESE DIP:
While the wings are baking, in a medium bowl, mash the blue cheese with the back of a fork until the cheese is finely broken up. Stir in the sour cream, chives, and lemon juice. Season with salt and pepper.

Serve the wings with the blue cheese dip and crudités.

PORK CRACKLING WITH COLESLAW, TROUT RILLETTES, AND SPICY RAPINI DIP

PREP 1 HOUR PLUS INITIAL COOK 1 HOUR × REFRIGERATE OVERNIGHT × COOK 12 HOURS × SERVES 8

Each recipe here stands on its own, but I like to serve them all together for my version of chips and dips. The pork crackling is worth the work, but if you prefer, go ahead and use store-bought pork rinds.

PORK CRACKLING

- **Pig skin from the belly, with a thin layer of fat, nipples trimmed off (ask your butcher for about half a belly's worth)**
- **Canola oil for deep-frying**
- **Smoked salt and freshly cracked black pepper**

Cook the pig skin in a stockpot of boiling water for 1 hour, until very soft. Drain and pat dry. Spread the skin, fat side up, on a baking sheet lined with a kitchen towel and refrigerate, uncovered, overnight.

Scrape all the fat from the skin. In a food dehydrator, dehydrate the skin for about 12 hours. It should be dry, crisp, and shiny like a piece of brown plastic. (Alternatively, transfer the skin to a baking sheet lined with parchment paper and bake at 170°F/75°C for 12 hours, or until dry and crisp.) (*Meanwhile, make the coleslaw, coleslaw dressing, trout rillettes, and rapini dip, if serving.*) In a deep-fryer or deep, heavy saucepan, heat 2 inches (5 cm) of canola oil to 350°F (180°C).

Break the skin into roughly 2-inch (5 cm) squares. Working in batches, fry until puffed, doubled in size, and crispy, about 15 seconds. Drain on paper towels and season with smoked salt and pepper. Break into large bite-size pieces.

COLESLAW

- **1/2 head napa cabbage, soaked in salted water for 2 hours, rinsed, drained, and shredded**
- **1/2 head green cabbage, shredded**
- **1 red onion, thinly sliced**
- **Leaves from a bunch of cilantro**
- **1 tablespoon (15 mL) chili flakes**
- **1/2 cup (125 mL) peanuts, toasted and crushed**

In a large bowl, combine the napa cabbage, green cabbage, red onion, cilantro, and chili flakes. Set aside.

COLESLAW DRESSING

- **1 tablespoon (15 mL) Dijon mustard**
- **1 tablespoon (15 mL) honey**
- **Zest and juice of 1 lemon**
- **1 garlic clove, minced**
- **1/2 cup (125 mL) olive oil**
- **Salt and freshly cracked black pepper**

In a small bowl, whisk together the mustard, honey, lemon zest and juice, and garlic. Whisking constantly, slowly add the olive oil, whisking until emulsified. Season with salt and pepper. Refrigerate until needed.

TROUT RILLETTES

- **1 skinless trout fillet (1/2 lb/ 225 g), cut in 4 pieces**
- **Salt and freshly cracked black pepper**
- **1 cup (250 mL) butter**
- **A sprig of thyme**
- **1 garlic clove, smashed**
- **1/4 cup (60 mL) crème fraîche**
- **1 small shallot, finely chopped**
- **Zest and juice of 1/2 lemon**
- **Finely chopped fresh chives, to taste**

- **Chopped fresh dill, to taste**
- **Toasted baguette or country loaf slices**
- **2 hard-boiled eggs**
- **Pickles, for serving**

Season the trout with salt and pepper.

In a saucepan, melt the butter over medium-high heat; add the thyme and garlic. Add the trout and cook for about 8 minutes or until flaky. Transfer the trout to a bowl, reserving the poaching butter, and let cool.

Using a fork, break the trout into small pieces. Add the crème fraîche and about 3 tablespoons (45 mL) of the poaching butter; stir with the fork, taking care not to mash the trout. Add the shallot, lemon zest and juice, chives, and dill. Season with salt and pepper. Spread on toasts. Grate the eggs over the rillettes. Serve with pickles.

SPICY RAPINI DIP
- **8 thin slices pancetta**
- **2 tablespoons (30 mL) olive oil, if needed**

- **1 lb (450 g) rapini, thick stems discarded, blanched**
- **3 tablespoons (45 mL) finely chopped store-bought pickled vegetables (antipasto calabrese or giardiniera)**
- **1 garlic clove, minced**
- **1 cup (250 mL) shredded Gruyère cheese**
- **1 cup (250 mL) cream cheese, softened**
- **1/2 cup (125 mL) whipping cream**
- **1 teaspoon (5 mL) chili flakes**
- **Salt and freshly cracked black pepper**
- **Toasts and assorted fresh vegetables**

In a large skillet, fry the pancetta until golden brown and crispy. Drain on paper towels and set aside. Heat the same skillet over medium-high heat. If necessary, add oil to the pancetta fat. Sauté the rapini, pickled vegetables, and garlic until the rapini is tender, 5 minutes. Reduce heat to low and add the Gruyère, cream cheese, and cream. Stir until melted and combined. Add the chili flakes and season with salt and

pepper. Transfer to a serving bowl and garnish with the crispy pancetta. Serve with toasts and assorted vegetables.

THE
CONCIERGES

Flank Steak Salad
Boston Salad with Fried Sardines
Braised Veal Cheeks with Waffles and Foie Gras
Dungeness Crab Salad with Crackers

One of the best things about Garde Manger is also what causes the most problems: our size. We're a pretty small place, and although I love our cozy, intimate atmosphere, sometimes it can make reservations a little tricky. We fill up quickly, and last-minute requests or concierges trying to get their hotel guests a table make for a bit of a juggling act.

Garde Manger is in Old Montreal, one of the most beautiful parts of the city. With all its historic charm, it's where many of the best hotels are located. Surrounded by all these hotels, we've had a chance to get to know many of the neighbourhood's concierges. These are the men and women who guide their guests when it comes to where to eat, where to shop, where to drink, and what to do. They know Montreal inside out, and they can make or break how a visitor sees our city.

The concierges try to send us customers they know will appreciate the style of food, service, and atmosphere that make Garde Manger special. Because we're so small, they know we can't accommodate everyone, so they have to decide who will be the best fit. We're not elitist in any way—we certainly don't choose our clientele—but we can't hide from the fact that our restaurant can get pretty loud, there's a lot of seafood on the menu, and it falls somewhere in between fine dining and rock and roll. That's a big part of the concierge's job: matching the customer with the destination. It's about accommodation, flexibility, and good customer service.

We want people to come to Garde Manger and have a good time. The concierges are there to please the hotel guests, and we want to do the same once they become our dinner guests. The hotel staff know that

the best clients to send us are the ones who really want to be here. We don't take it for granted that Montreal is a city full of amazing restaurants. Concierges have their pick of the litter when it comes to places to send their guests. When we get that phone call, we're honoured that they thought of us and we know we need to find that table.

We appreciate working with the concierges because it gives us a direct link to the customer. If you call us or make a reservation online, we know just three things: a name, a time, and how many people are dining. If we get a call from a hotel, however, it's a different story. We find out where you're from, why you're in Montreal, if it's your first time, if you have any allergies, if it's a special celebration. It helps us to fine-tune your dining experience and make it all the better.

The concierges not only support our restaurant, but they give us the tools to go above and beyond. When a customer returns to the hotel after an amazing dinner with us, we've all done a good job.

FLANK STEAK SALAD

PREP 20 MIN × COOK 10 MIN × SERVES 6

Flank steak is a great cut of meat because it's inexpensive and tastes amazing. Don't hold back on the seasoning to bring out all its natural flavour.

- 1 flank steak (2 lb/900 g)
- Salt and freshly cracked black pepper
- 1 tablespoon (15 mL) canola oil
- 1 red onion, sliced
- 2 cucumbers, cut in 1-inch pieces
- 2 tomatoes, diced
- 2 avocados, halved, pitted, and diced
- A handful of fresh cilantro leaves
- A handful of fresh mint leaves
- Juice of 2 limes
- 2 tablespoons (30 mL) olive oil

Season the steak on both sides with salt and pepper. Heat the oil in a large, heavy skillet over high heat until hot but not smoking. Cook the steak on one side for 5 minutes. Flip and cook on the other side for 5 more minutes for medium-rare. Transfer to a plate and cover loosely with foil to keep warm.

Meanwhile, in a medium bowl, combine the onion, cucumbers, tomatoes, avocados, cilantro, mint, lime juice, and olive oil. Toss well. Season with salt and pepper.

To serve, slice the flank steak and divide among plates. Pile the salad on top.

BOSTON SALAD WITH FRIED SARDINES

PREP 15 MIN × COOK 10 MIN × SERVES 4

This salad is a popular menu item at Garde Manger. We stack layers of lettuce and fried sardines and then crumble crispy speck on top for that extra crunch.

DRESSING
- 1/4 cup (60 mL) mayonnaise
- 2 tablespoons (30 mL) sour cream
- 1 tablespoon (15 mL) red wine vinegar
- 1 tablespoon (15 mL) finely chopped fresh tarragon
- 1 tablespoon (15 mL) finely chopped fresh chervil
- 1 shallot, finely chopped
- 1 clove roasted garlic (page 150)
- Juice of 1/2 lemon
- Salt and freshly cracked black pepper

SPECK
- 3 tablespoons (45 mL) olive oil
- 8 thin slices speck or pancetta

FRIED SARDINES
- Canola oil for deep-frying
- 1 cup (250 mL) all-purpose flour, plus more for dredging
- 1/4 cup (60 mL) cornstarch
- 1 tablespoon (15 mL) baking powder
- Salt and freshly cracked black pepper
- 2 eggs
- 1½ cups (375 mL) beer
- 16 fresh sardine fillets

FOR SERVING
- 1 head Boston lettuce

FOR THE DRESSING:
In a small bowl, combine the mayonnaise, sour cream, vinegar, tarragon, chervil, shallot, garlic, and lemon juice; stir well. Season with salt and pepper. Set aside.

FOR THE SPECK:
Heat the oil in a large skillet over medium heat. Fry the speck until crispy. Drain on paper towels and set aside.

FOR THE FRIED SARDINES:
In a deep-fryer or deep, heavy saucepan, heat 2 inches (5 cm) of canola oil to 350°F (180°C).

In a medium bowl, whisk together the flour, cornstarch, and baking powder. Season with salt and pepper.

In another bowl, beat the eggs. Stir in the beer. Add to the flour mixture and stir just until combined (don't worry about a few lumps).

Working in batches, dredge the sardine fillets in flour. Dip into the beer batter, letting excess drip off. Fry until crisp and golden brown, about 1½ minutes, turning halfway. Drain on paper towels and season with salt and pepper.

To serve, on each plate, layer the fried sardines between lettuce leaves, drizzling each leaf with a little dressing. Crumble the speck on top.

BRAISED VEAL CHEEKS WITH WAFFLES AND FOIE GRAS

PREP 30 MIN × COOK 2 HOURS 45 MIN × SERVES 4

If you've never tried veal cheeks, here's your chance to give it a shot. I promise you this melt-in-your-mouth meat will make you an instant convert.

BRAISED VEAL CHEEKS

- 1 tablespoon (15 mL) canola oil
- 8 veal cheeks (about 3 lb/ 1.35 kg)
- Salt and freshly cracked black pepper
- 1 onion, chopped
- 1 carrot, chopped
- 1 celery rib, chopped
- 1 head of garlic, halved crosswise
- 6 cups (1.5 L) veal stock
- 2 cups (500 mL) braising liquid
- 1 cup (250 mL) beer
- 3 tablespoons (45 mL) maple syrup
- 2 tablespoons (30 mL) cold butter, cubed
- Salt and freshly cracked black pepper

WAFFLES

- 1½ cups (375 mL) all-purpose flour
- 1 tablespoon (15 mL) baking powder
- A pinch of salt
- 3 large eggs, separated
- 2 cups (500 mL) sour cream
- 1/2 cup (125 mL) milk
- 1/4 cup (60 mL) butter, melted

FOIE GRAS

- 4 slices grade A duck foie gras
- Salt and freshly cracked black pepper
- 1 tablespoon (15 mL) butter

GARNISH

- Bibb lettuce leaves
- Maldon sea salt and freshly cracked black pepper

FOR THE BRAISED VEAL CHEEKS:
Preheat oven to 350°F (180°C).

In a large braising pot or Dutch oven, heat the oil over medium-high heat until hot but not smoking. Season the veal cheeks with salt and pepper. Sear them in the hot oil until golden brown on each side, about 5 minutes. Add the onion, carrot, and celery; continue cooking for 5 minutes. Add the garlic and veal stock. Cover, transfer to the oven, and braise for 2 hours or until the meat is fork-tender. Transfer the veal to a plate and cover with foil to keep warm.

Strain the braising liquid into a bowl; skim off excess fat. Measure 2 cups (500 mL) into a saucepan. Bring to a boil and reduce by half, about 20 minutes; reduce heat to medium-low. Meanwhile, in a small saucepan, boil the beer until reduced by half, about 20 minutes. Add the beer to the reduced braising liquid; add the maple syrup. Whisk in the butter, a few pieces at a time. Season with salt and pepper. Remove the sauce from heat and keep warm.

FOR THE WAFFLES:
Preheat oven to 200°F (100°C).

In a large bowl, whisk together the flour, baking powder, and salt. In a medium bowl, beat the egg whites until soft peaks form; set aside. In another bowl, beat the egg yolks. Stir in the sour cream, milk, and melted butter. Add to the dry ingredients, stirring just until combined (a few lumps are okay). Gently but thoroughly fold in the egg whites.

Heat a waffle iron. Pour in the batter (a generous 1/2 cup/125 mL for each waffle) and cook the waffles for about 5 minutes or until golden brown and cooked through. Transfer to rack in oven to keep warm. Repeat with the remaining batter.

FOR THE FOIE GRAS:
Heat a large cast-iron pan on high heat until very hot. Season the foie gras with salt and pepper. Sear just until golden brown on each side, about 20 seconds per side. Spoon the butter over the foie gras; remove from heat.

To serve, place a waffle on each plate. Top each waffle with 2 braised veal cheeks. Add a ladle of the sauce. Top with a slice of foie gras and some Bibb lettuce. Season with Maldon salt and pepper.

DUNGENESS CRAB SALAD with CRACKERS

PREP 30 MIN PLUS 2 HOURS FOR RISING × COOK 25 MIN × SERVES 4

Nothing beats freshly cooked crab-meat, and if you've ever cooked lobster at home, then there's no need to fear Dungeness crab. The mixed herb salad complements the crab's slightly sweet, delicate taste with a bit of heat from the bird's eye chili.

CRACKERS (MAKES ABOUT 50 CRACKERS)

- 4 cups (1 L) warm water
- 1/4 cup (60 mL) extra-virgin olive oil
- 1 tablespoon (15 mL) active dry yeast
- 1 tablespoon (15 mL) sugar
- 1 tablespoon (15 mL) sea salt
- About 8 cups (2 L) all-purpose flour
- Sesame seeds and/or coarse salt and freshly cracked black pepper

DUNGENESS CRAB SALAD

- 1/2 cup (125 mL) coarse salt
- 1 bottle (2 oz/57 mL) hot pepper sauce
- 4 live Dungeness crabs
- 1 bird's eye chili, finely chopped
- A handful of fresh chives, minced
- A handful of celery leaves
- 2 tablespoons (30 mL) olive oil
- Zest and juice of 1 lemon
- 4 large croutons, crushed
- Maldon sea salt and freshly cracked black pepper

FOR THE CRACKERS:

In the bowl of a stand mixer fitted with the dough hook, stir together the water, olive oil, yeast, sugar, and salt. Let rest for 5 minutes or until foamy. Add the flour. Knead on medium speed for 5 minutes or until the dough forms a ball. (You can also knead the dough by hand on a floured surface.)

Shape the dough into a ball and place it in a lightly oiled bowl. Cover with plastic wrap and let sit at room temperature for 2 hours or until doubled in size (or refrigerate overnight).

Preheat oven to 400°F (200°C). Line a baking sheet with parchment paper.

Divide the dough in half. On a lightly floured surface, roll out one half very thinly. Cut the dough into long strips and arrange them on the baking sheet close together but not touching. Mist with water and sprinkle with sesame seeds and/or coarse salt and pepper.

Bake for 10 minutes or until golden all over. Cool before serving. (*Crackers keep, in an airtight container at room temperature, for 2 weeks.*)

FOR THE DUNGENESS CRAB SALAD:

Bring a large pot of water to a boil. Add the coarse salt and hot pepper sauce. Add the crabs and cook for about 15 minutes. Drain nose end down and let cool.

Peel off and discard the tail. Pull off the legs and claws; set aside. Place each crab on its belly. Push your thumb in where the tail was; grab the top shell in your other hand and peel it off. (You can also use a knife to lever the crab apart.) Drain any excess water from the shell. Discard the eyes, gills, stomach sac, and hard membranes inside the shell. Spoon the meat into a bowl. Clean the top shell; set aside. Crack open the claws and legs and pick out the meat; add to the bowl. Pick through the meat and discard any remaining bits of membrane or shell.

Add the chili, chives, celery leaves, olive oil, lemon zest and juice, and croutons; stir to combine. Season with Maldon salt and pepper. Spoon the salad into the cleaned shells. Serve with the crackers.

STAFF MEAL

FISH BOLOGNESE
GARBAGE SALAD
"HOT DOG" RISOTTO
CLASSIC HANGER STEAK AND FRIES
CHOCOLATE STOUT CAKE WITH ORANGE CUSTARD SAUCE

When we opened Garde Manger we had this amazing idea: we would have a dish called Staff Meal on the menu. It was about $10 and would be exactly what the staff had that night for dinner. It was always a bit of a gamble because it changed every night, but it was the cheapest dish we offered. As much as we all loved this concept, it *was* a little strange, and needless to say, Staff Meal as a menu item was short-lived. But actual staff meal? That's a daily essential.

Around five every afternoon, without fail, the kitchen prepares a dinner for everyone who is working that night. The prep cooks start their day at 9 a.m., and by noon we usually have a full kitchen. The wait staff come in anywhere after three, and everyone works late, some until three or four in the morning. It's a long and tiring stretch. Everyone works their butts off, and they deserve to eat a proper meal.

Not only is this important for the most obvious reason (to eat), but having a meal together, made by the staff for the staff, gives us a chance to communicate and also relax a bit before the storm hits. It also gives me the opportunity to have a meeting before the doors open and do what I like to call a little ship, shape, and shine pre-service.

Just like every day in the restaurant, every staff meal is different. Some days there's something good, and other days it's . . . okay. The point is to make the best with what we have. The bottom line is to eat; it's not about having a culinary adventure every time, but if we can make it fun and filling, that's great. Basically it's meant to be cost efficient and nourishing because working here is a sport. I want to serve stuff with carbs, usually pasta, greens, and if we can throw some meat in there, perfect.

Staff meal challenges the kitchen to come up with something new while trying to get rid of stuff we don't need. If we're trying out a new recipe and it isn't quite right yet, it becomes a part of staff meal. If someone's dessert experiment is an epic fail, it becomes part of staff meal too—and trust me, no one will complain about that. When the kitchen takes the time and puts in the extra effort, it's really appreciated and sets the tone for the evening. Staff meal is a blend of necessity and saying, "Thanks, guys. Now let's hammer it out tonight and don't forget to have a good time."

Feed the people and they'll be happy. It's such a basic idea, and it reflects how much we care about our staff. Here is a menu of some of our staff meal greatest hits.

FISH BOLOGNESE

PREP 15 MIN × COOK 20 MIN × SERVES 4 TO 6

This fish bolognese came to be because we serve a lot of seafood in the restaurant—salmon, tuna, halibut, it's a real melting pot. We trim everything, so there are all sorts of good bits left over. We throw everything into a tomato sauce and it all blends together for a hearty, healthy pasta sauce.

- 3 tablespoons (45 mL) olive oil
- 1/2 lb (225 g) cured chorizo, diced
- 1 onion, minced
- 4 garlic cloves, minced
- 1½ lb (675 g) white-fleshed fish (halibut, cod, walleye, sole, mackerel, etc.)
- 2 cups (500 mL) fish, chicken, or veal stock
- 12 cherry tomatoes, halved (or about 2 cups/500 mL tomato sauce)
- 1/2 cup (125 mL) pitted oil-cured black olives
- 1/4 cup (60 mL) large salt-cured capers, rinsed
- Chili flakes, to taste
- 1 lb (450 g) rigatoni
- 1/4 cup (60 mL) chopped fresh parsley
- 1/4 cup (60 mL) chopped fresh chives
- Salt and freshly cracked black pepper
- 1/2 cup (125 mL) grated Parmigiano-Reggiano cheese

Heat the oil in a large skillet over medium heat. Add the chorizo; cook until crispy. Add the onion and garlic; cook until the onion is soft. Add the fish; continue cooking, breaking up the fish into flakes with a wooden spoon. Add the stock, cherry tomatoes, olives, capers, and chili flakes. Simmer, stirring occasionally, for about 10 minutes. Remove from heat.

Meanwhile, cook the rigatoni until al dente. Drain the pasta and add it to the sauce; add the parsley and chives. Toss well over low heat.

Season with salt, black pepper, and more chili flakes, if desired.

To serve, transfer to a serving bowl and top with the Parmesan.

GARBAGE SALAD

PREP 15 MIN × SERVES 8

I know something called Garbage Salad doesn't sound appealing, but it was inspired by something we used to make in cooking school called potage garbure, or basically garbage soup. You take everything that you have on hand, vegetables, herbs, whatever's lying around, and turn it into a creamy stew or purée. At the restaurant, we apply the idea to a salad. On any given night we'll have ingredients left over from the night before—cherry tomatoes, asparagus spears, cucumbers, herbs, maybe some smoked salmon, maybe some cheese—sometimes the combinations are more random than others, and it's never the same! Everything we serve to our guests is fresh that day, but if something is a day old, the staff gets it. It's a healthy way to clean out the fridge.

SALAD

- 8 cups (2 L) mixed greens (spinach, arugula, etc.)
- 1/2 lb (225 g) green beans, blanched
- About 12 asparagus spears, blanched and chopped
- 1 tomato, chopped
- Tomato caps, chopped
- Tops and bottoms of red bell peppers, chopped
- 1 shallot, thinly sliced
- A handful of chopped or whole mixed fresh herbs (chives, parsley, tarragon, celery leaves, etc.)

DRESSING

- 3 tablespoons (45 mL) olive oil
- 1 tablespoon (15 mL) white balsamic vinegar
- Coarse salt and freshly cracked black pepper

GARNISHES

- Croutons, smoked chips, shoestring potatoes, fried shallots, etc.
- Smoked salmon trimmings
- Grilled hanger steak trimmings

FOR THE SALAD:

In a large bowl, combine all the ingredients.

FOR THE DRESSING:

Whisk together the olive oil and vinegar. Season with coarse salt and pepper.

To serve, toss the salad with the dressing. Top with the garnishes.

"HOT DOG" RISOTTO

PREP 30 MIN × COOK 22 MIN × SERVES 6

"Hot dog" risotto isn't exactly what it sounds like. All we had one day for staff meal was risotto, gnocchi, and some sausages. The boys called it "Hot Dog" Risotto, and it was such a hit that the name stuck. We use any kind of sausage we have on hand—store-bought, homemade, whatever. This recipe uses pepper-ette, but you can use whatever you like—even good-quality hot dogs. Whatever you go with, this dish is addictively good.

RISOTTO

- 1 onion, finely chopped
- 1 tablespoon (15 mL) olive oil
- 2 cups (500 mL) arborio rice
- 4 cups (1 L) water
- 1/4 cup (60 mL) butter, cubed
- 1 cup (250 mL) grated Parmi-giano-Reggiano cheese
- Salt and freshly cracked black pepper

RICOTTA GNOCCHI

- 2 cups (500 mL) ricotta cheese
- 1/2 cup (125 mL) grated Parmigiano-Reggiano cheese
- 1/2 cup (125 mL) finely chopped fresh chives
- 1 teaspoon (5 mL) salt
- 2 large eggs, beaten
- 1/2 head of roasted garlic (page 150)
- Salt and freshly cracked black pepper
- About 3 cups (750 mL) all-purpose flour

GARNISHES

- 1 tablespoon (15 mL) canola oil
- 1/2 lb (225 g) pepperette, chopped (or 2 large cooked sausages, sliced)
- 1 shallot, minced
- 2 garlic cloves, minced
- 1 red bell pepper, roasted, peeled, seeded, and chopped
- 1 cup (250 mL) chicken stock
- A handful of chopped or whole mixed fresh herbs (parsley, chives, celery leaves, etc.)
- Grated Parmigiano-Reggiano cheese
- Salt and freshly cracked black pepper

FOR THE RISOTTO:

In a large saucepan over medium-high heat, sauté the onion in the oil until translucent. Stir in the rice; cook, stirring constantly, for 2 minutes. Add 1 cup (250 mL) of the water; continue cooking on medium heat, stirring constantly, until the liquid is almost all absorbed. Continue adding water, 1 cup (250 mL) at a time, stirring until each addition is absorbed before adding more, until the rice is tender and creamy but still al dente, about 20 minutes. Stir in the butter and Parmesan. Season with salt and pepper. Remove from heat and keep warm.

FOR RICOTTA GNOCCHI:

In a food processor, combine the ricotta, Parmesan, chives, salt, eggs, and garlic. Season with salt and pepper. Process to mix. Add the flour and pulse just until a soft dough forms. Do not overmix.

Divide the dough into quarters. Roll each piece into a log 1 inch (2.5 cm) wide. Cut into 1-inch (2.5 cm) cylinders.

Bring a large pot of salted water to a boil. Cook gnocchi for 2 minutes or until they float. Using a slotted spoon, transfer them to a bowl of ice water to stop the cooking. Drain before using.

FOR THE GARNISHES:

In a large skillet, heat the oil over medium-high heat. Sauté the pepperette until browned, about 5 minutes. Add the shallot and gar-lic; continue cooking for 2 minutes. Add the red pepper, risotto, gnocchi, and stock. Continue cooking to heat through. Remove from heat and stir in the herbs and Parmesan. Season with salt and pepper.

CLASSIC HANGER STEAK AND FRIES

PREP 15 MIN PLUS 6 HOURS FOR MARINATING × COOK 10 MIN × SERVES 4

One thing we always have on the menu, without fail, is classic hanger steak and fries. So the staff is pretty happy when we have a couple of extra steaks kicking around. If they had a say, this would be staff meal all the time, but I don't need a staff weighing in at a collective six tons. Once in a while, though, this classic is always welcome.

HANGER STEAKS
- 1/4 cup (60 mL) olive oil
- 2 tablespoons (30 mL) red wine vinegar
- 1 garlic clove, minced
- Leaves from 2 sprigs of rosemary, minced
- Leaves from 2 sprigs of thyme, minced
- 4 hanger steaks (about 1/2 lb/225 g each)
- 3 tablespoons (45 mL) canola oil
- 2 tablespoons (30 mL) steak spice

FRIES
- Canola oil for deep-frying
- 6 Yukon Gold potatoes, cut in matchsticks
- Salt and freshly cracked black pepper
- Homemade mayonnaise (page 46), for serving

FOR THE HANGER STEAKS:
In a small bowl, whisk together the olive oil, vinegar, garlic, rosemary, and thyme. Place the steaks in a nonaluminum dish just large enough to hold them in one layer. Pour the marinade over the steaks. Cover and refrigerate at least 6 hours or overnight.

In a large cast-iron skillet, heat the canola oil over high heat. Remove the steaks from the marinade (discarding the marinade); rub them all over with the steak spice. Cook the steaks, without moving them in the pan, for 4 minutes on one side. Flip and continue cooking on the other side for about 2 minutes for rare. Transfer to a warm platter, cover loosely with foil, and let rest for about 5 minutes.

FOR THE FRIES:
In a deep-fryer or deep, heavy saucepan, heat 2 inches (5 cm) of canola oil to 250°F (120°C).

Working in batches, fry the potatoes for 2 to 3 minutes; do not let them colour. Drain on paper towels and let rest a couple of minutes.

Heat the oil to 350°F (180°C). Fry the potatoes again until golden brown and crispy. Drain on paper towels. Season with salt and pepper.

Serve the steaks with the fries and mayo.

COOK'S NOTE:
At the restaurant, we blanch our fries at the beginning of the day. Then we can fry them the second time at the last minute. Any that aren't used for guests get cooked up the next day for staff meal—and we've found they're even tastier after they've soaked up some fat overnight.

CHOCOLATE STOUT CAKE WITH ORANGE CUSTARD SAUCE

PREP 25 MIN PLUS 12 HOURS FOR SOAKING × COOK 50 MIN × SERVES 4

Sometimes we have chocolate stout cake on the menu. We make it in a big rectangular pan and cut out circles to serve to customers. Whatever is left is what my staff gets, and it seems as if the trimmings somehow keep getting bigger and bigger! If you can manage to serve a dessert with staff meal you get a lot of props, no matter what it looks like.

ORANGES WITH COGNAC
- 3 oranges
- 1/4 cup (60 mL) sugar
- 3 tablespoons (45 mL) cognac
- 1 vanilla bean

ORANGE CUSTARD SAUCE
- 1/2 cup (125 mL) milk
- 1/2 cup (125 mL) whipping cream
- 1 vanilla bean
- 3 large egg yolks
- 1/4 cup (60 mL) sugar
- A pinch of salt
- Zest and juice of 1 orange

CHOCOLATE STOUT CAKE
- 1½ cups (375 mL) stout beer
- 1/2 cup (125 mL) whipping cream
- 1/2 cup (125 mL) + 2 table-spoons (30 mL) sugar
- 1¼ cups (310 mL) chopped bittersweet chocolate
- 4 large eggs

- 2 teaspoons (10 mL) vanilla extract
- 4 cups (1 L) 1-inch (2.5 cm) cubes brioche bread with crust

FOR THE ORANGES WITH COGNAC:
Juice 1 orange; set aside juice. Thinly slice the remaining 2 oranges crosswise, removing any seeds; place the slices in a medium bowl.

In a small saucepan, combine the sugar, cognac, and reserved orange juice. Scrape the seeds from the vanilla bean into the pan, then add the pod. Heat the mixture over medium heat, stirring occasionally, until the sugar is dissolved, about 2 minutes. Pour over the orange slices. Cover and refrigerate for at least 12 hours.

FOR THE ORANGE CUSTARD SAUCE:
In a small saucepan, combine the milk and cream. Scrape the seeds from the vanilla bean into the pan, then add the pod. Bring to a boil. Remove from heat and discard the vanilla pod.

In a medium bowl, whisk together the egg yolks, sugar, and salt until thick, about 2 minutes, then gradually whisk in the hot milk mixture. Return the mixture to the saucepan and cook over medium-low heat, stirring constantly with a wooden spoon, until the custard is thick

enough to coat the back of the spoon, 4 to 6 minutes. Do not let boil. Strain the custard through a fine-mesh sieve into a bowl; stir in the orange zest and juice. Cover the surface with plastic wrap, let cool to room temperature, then refrigerate.

FOR THE CHOCOLATE STOUT CAKE:
Preheat oven to 325°F (160°C). Butter an 8-inch (2 L) baking pan.

Bring the stout, cream, and 1/2 cup (125 mL) sugar to a simmer in a medium saucepan, stirring until the sugar is dissolved. Remove from heat. Add 1 cup (250 mL) of the chocolate and whisk until melted and smooth. Set aside to cool.

In a large bowl, whisk the eggs with the vanilla. Gradually whisk in the cooled chocolate mixture. Add the bread cubes and the remaining 1/4 cup (60 mL) chocolate; toss to coat. Transfer to the cake pan. Sprinkle with the remaining 2 table-spoons (30 mL) sugar. Bake until the custard thickens and the centre is just set, 50 to 60 minutes.

To serve, using a 4-inch (10 cm) round biscuit cutter, cut out circles of warm cake. Arrange on plates. Pour the orange custard sauce over the cake and garnish with drained orange slices.

LIFE

Cooking is very revealing—there's no hiding behind your food. When you're in charge of the kitchen, you're constantly putting yourself out there to be scrutinized and judged by everyone who walks in that door. There's a saying in the restaurant business, and it might sound like a cliché but from my experience it's true: you're only as good as your last dish. As a chef, that's what motivates me every night. When it comes down to it, no matter what anyone says about me, the proof is on the plate.

It's hard to not always take my work personally and to stay focused and grounded. That's because so much of my personality is in the food I make and so much of my heart is in the restaurant. That's where those closest to me come in, the people who get me out of my own head, remind me about the important things in life, remind me that there's more to it than just cooking.

Sometimes that line between work and life gets blurred because I spend so much of my time at the restaurant. It's my home away from home, and although I love Garde Manger, it's not healthy to never stop and come up for air. A lot of important people in my life are part of my work life, and I'm thankful for that because they have been able to help me through the tough times when I needed them the most. They're the people I go to with problems and listen to for advice, but they're also the people I hang out with, have fun with, and most important, forget about work with.

Whether I see these special people every day, every week, or once a year, I know they'll always be there for me. From my family to Safwan, my tattoo artist, the guys I cater music festivals for in the summer, and the girls who tried to walk my dog, from my hockey teams and my trainer, Alex, to the couple at the sandwich shop in my neighbourhood and the regular clients at the restaurant, these people all help keep me grounded. Cooking keeps me on my toes at work, but these people keep me on my toes all the time.

My Family

Nothing means more to me than impressing my family. They're the ones I get nervous cooking for because with them, there's no holding back   if they don't like something, they're definitely going to let me know, and they won't sugar-coat it. On top of that, they're the ones who encouraged me to follow my passion for food and helped me to get where I am today.

When I was ten, I asked my mom if I could take cooking classes at my school. (Okay, okay, being the only guy in a class full of girls might have had something to do with it, but hey, everyone starts somewhere.) After being in the class for a little while, I thought I'd surprise my mom with a homemade apple pie. She took one bite and told me it was great, but I could tell by the look on her face that maybe she wasn't so sure about that. Years later, when I told her I wanted to go to cooking school, she said it was a wonderful idea, but in the back of her mind I guarantee you she was still thinking about that pie.

No one has had a bigger influence on me than my mom, Francine. She was a stewardess, and one of my best food memories was when she would fly back from the East Coast with huge bags stuffed with seafood—lobster, shrimp, crab, you name it. My mom, my grandmother, and I would just sit there and devour all that fresh, delicious seafood together. I still associate these foods with growing up, family, and comfort. When we opened Garde Manger and needed someone to do desserts, my mom was the first one to step up to the plate. (Was she still thinking about that pie? Still?)

It was always my mom's dream to be a chef. She opened a restaurant in St-Sauveur, Quebec, in 1982, but it just didn't work out and it closed shortly after. I think her drive to succeed in the industry was what she passed down to me. I don't think she realized it at the time, but teaching me everything she knew about food, cooking, focus, and discipline would prepare me for the very difficult road ahead. Without her encouragement to push further and aim higher, I don't know if I would have come this far. My success is just as much hers too.

I should mention that besides my mom, everyone in my family cooks, from my aunt Danie and my cousins Ben and Phil to my girlfriend, Sabrina. Well, everyone except my dad, Pierre. He's just a very good eater! But he also tends to keep the peace when arguments arise. We all have our own opinion, and things can get pretty heated in the kitchen at family gatherings.

You might think that if I were cooking for my family, I would do it in the comfort of my own home, but I have a little confession to make: in my home kitchen, I'm totally lost. I tend to order takeout. A lot. Okay, way more than I should. At home I go to reach for things that aren't there, I miss my favourite pan, I miss the high heat of my gas stove. In my restaurant kitchen, though, I'm on fire—I can move fast, I know where everything is, and I'm completely in my element. As much as the restaurant kitchen is my home turf, the home kitchen is Sabrina's.

The love of food is a common thread with all of those close to me. I first met Sabrina at the restaurant. She would come in every Wednesday, sit at the bar, and have a couple dozen oysters to herself. This definitely piqued my interest. When we started talking, she invited me to a party after work, but I told her I was going to the Main, a famous old-time Montreal deli, to have some chopped liver. Her eyes widened with excitement. "Chopped liver?" And the rest is pretty much history.

Sabrina's Russian-Jewish background means that food is in her blood. Not only does she appreciate good food (I mean, c'mon, we met in my restaurant!), but she's an amazing cook and makes all these incredible recipes passed down in her family. Her cooking inspires me, and we value the same things in life, so really, she's the perfect fit.

Contrary to what you might think, my family doesn't come and eat in the restaurant that often, because they know it stresses me out. When I'm in that kitchen, I'm at work. I get in the zone, put my head down, and just go until the very last plate is out. I'd love to walk away from the line, sit and relax with the people I care about, but I just can't handle it.

In this industry it's hard to spend as much time as I would like with loved ones, so when I do cook for my family, it gives me a chance to show them how grateful I am that they've put up with so much over the years—missed birthday parties and cancelled plans, my not being there for vacations or weekends.

It's difficult to put into words the importance of family in my life, so I'm just going to do what I know best: cook from the heart. I know it's cheesy, but it's true. Inspired by those I care about most, this menu is more than just food to put on the table.

CHEESE AND TOMATO TART

PREP 15 MIN × COOK 25 MIN × SERVES 8

My aunt Danie used to make us this tart, and I often crave it. It's best with fresh tomatoes and herbs in summer. You can prepare it ahead and serve it cold, or pop it in the oven to heat up right before you eat.

- 8 sheets phyllo pastry, thawed
- 1/4 cup (60 mL) butter, melted
- 2 tablespoons (30 mL) Dijon mustard
- 2 cups (500 mL) shredded Emmental cheese
- 8 large ripe tomatoes, sliced 1/4 inch (5 mm) thick
- Coarse salt and freshly cracked black pepper
- 1 tablespoon (15 mL) fresh thyme leaves
- 12 fresh basil leaves for garnish

Preheat oven to 400°F (200°C).

Lay 1 phyllo sheet in a large baking sheet, leaving a slight overhang at the edges. (Keep remaining phyllo covered with a damp cloth so it doesn't dry out.) Brush phyllo with some melted butter. Repeat with the remaining phyllo and butter, stacking sheets on top of each other and overlapping so the baking sheet is well covered and leaving a little bit of an edge.

Brush phyllo with the mustard. Sprinkle the cheese evenly over the pastry. Arrange the tomato slices over the cheese, overlapping slightly. Season with salt and pepper. Sprinkle with the thyme leaves. Bake until the pastry is crisp and browned at the edges, about 25 minutes.

Add another sprinkling of coarse salt. Cut the tart into 8 squares. Garnish with fresh basil leaves.

Delicious served hot, warm, or at room temperature.

WARM MUSHROOM AND SPECK SALAD
ON GOAT CHEESE BRIOCHE

PREP 3 MIN × COOK 6 MIN × SERVES 8

I love mushrooms, and in this recipe you can throw in any kind you like. The mushrooms are great served warm or at room temperature.

BRIOCHE (MAKES 2 LOAVES)
PREP 20 MIN PLUS 3 HOURS RISING TIME × COOK 40 MIN

- 1/4 cup (60 mL) warm water (110°F/43°C)
- 1 tablespoon (15 mL) sugar
- 1 tablespoon (15 mL) active dry yeast
- 6 large eggs, at room temperature
- 5 cups (1.25 L) all-purpose flour
- 2 teaspoons (10 mL) salt
- 1 cup (250 mL) butter, softened
- Egg wash (1 egg yolk beaten with 1 tablespoon/15 mL milk)

WARM MUSHROOM AND SPECK SALAD

- 2 lb (900 g) assorted mushrooms (king oyster, shiitake, portobello, chanterelle, lobster, baby button, etc.)
- 2 tablespoons (30 mL) butter
- 2 tablespoons (30 mL) olive oil
- Coarse salt and freshly cracked black pepper
- 1/3 cup (75 mL) chicken stock
- 1 cup (250 mL) pitted mixed olives
- Leaves from 1/2 bunch oregano

GARNISHES

- 1 cup (250 mL) soft goat cheese
- 8 thin slices speck or pancetta

FOR THE BRIOCHE:

In a small bowl, stir together the water, sugar, and yeast. Set aside for 5 minutes or until the mixture is foamy.

In a bowl, beat the eggs until they are frothy. Beat in the yeast mixture. Beat in about 1/2 cup (125 mL) of the flour and the salt, then beat in a couple of tablespoons (30 mL) of butter; continue alternately beating in flour and butter until the dough is firm enough to handle. Transfer it to a floured work surface and knead, adding any remaining flour if needed, until the dough is very elastic and smooth but still somewhat soft and sticky.

Butter a large bowl. Place the dough in the bowl, cover with plastic wrap, and set aside for 2 hours or until doubled in size.

Butter 2 loaf pans, line with parchment paper, and butter the paper. Punch the dough down and divide it in half. Shape each piece into a fat cylinder and fit into the pans. Cover with plastic wrap and let sit for another hour or until doubled in size.

Preheat oven to 400°F (200°C).

Brush the loaves with the egg wash. Bake for about 40 minutes, until the loaves are golden brown. Place the pans on a rack and let cool for 10 minutes. Turn the loaves out of the pans and let cool completely.

FOR THE SALAD:

Trim and clean the mushrooms. (Remove the stems from shiitakes and portobellos. Using a spoon, scrape the black gills from the portobellos so they won't blacken the mixture. Wash lobster mushrooms well in water.) Tear or cut into slices or chunks the larger mushrooms; small mushrooms are good left whole. Keep it rustic.

In a large skillet over medium-high heat, melt the butter in the oil in a large skillet over medium-high heat. When the butter is sizzling, add the mushrooms. Cook, tossing occasionally, for 6 to 8 minutes or until the edges are golden. Season with salt and pepper. Deglaze with the chicken stock, stirring to meld the flavours and glaze the mushrooms. Add the olives and oregano; toss.

To serve, grill slices of brioche. Spread with goat cheese. Spoon the mushrooms over the toast and garnish with slices of speck.

MARTINI PORK CHOPS

PREP 5 MIN × COOK 15 MIN × SERVES 8

My dad's nickname for me used to be Pork Chops, so this recipe always reminds me of him. It's super-simple and always good. If you don't have vermouth on hand, you can use white wine or even veal stock.

- 8 pork chops (1 to 1 ½ inches/2.5 to 4 cm thick)
- Coarse salt and freshly cracked black pepper
- 3 tablespoons (45 mL) butter
- 1 tablespoon (15 mL) olive oil
- 2 large shallots, sliced lengthwise
- 1/2 to 3/4 cup (125 to 175 mL) dry vermouth

Season the pork chops with salt and pepper.

In a large skillet over high heat, melt 1 tablespoon (15 mL) of the butter in the oil. Add the pork chops and sear them for about 3 minutes on each side. Reduce heat to medium and continue cooking until the chops are cooked through but still moist, about 6 more minutes, depending on the thickness of your chops.

Transfer the chops to a platter and cover with foil to keep warm. Pour off excess fat from the pan, return pan to heat, and add the shallots; cook, stirring, a few minutes, until they soften. Add the vermouth, stirring to scrape up all the browned bits. Simmer the sauce for a minute or two until reduced slightly. Stir in a generous nub of butter. Drizzle over the pork chops.

ROASTED PEACH CRUMBLE

PREP 15 MIN × COOK 15 MIN × SERVES 8

This dish is amazing when peaches are in season. The crumble on its own is a great snack and can be eaten on yogurt or ice cream or, like I do, by the handful.

CRUMBLE
- 1 cup (250 mL) old-fashioned rolled oats
- 1/2 cup (125 mL) sliced almonds, toasted
- 1/2 cup (125 mL) brown sugar
- 1/2 cup (125 mL) all-purpose flour
- 1/2 cup (125 mL) butter, melted
- 1 teaspoon (5 mL) cinnamon
- 1 teaspoon (5 mL) Maldon sea salt

PAN-ROASTED PEACHES
- 2 tablespoons (30 mL) butter
- 8 peaches, halved and pitted
- 1/4 cup (60 mL) maple syrup

FOR SERVING
- Vanilla ice cream
- A drizzle of Balconville vinegar (see page 65) or good-quality balsamic vinegar

FOR THE CRUMBLE:
Preheat oven to 350°F (180°C). Line a baking sheet with parchment paper.

In a large bowl, combine the oats, almonds, brown sugar, flour, melted butter, cinnamon, and salt. Rub with your fingers until the mixture resembles coarse crumbs. Spread in an even layer on the baking sheet. Bake for 10 minutes or until golden brown. Set aside.

FOR THE PAN-ROASTED PEACHES:
In a large skillet, melt the butter over medium-high heat. Add the peaches cut side down. Cook until golden brown on the bottom, about 5 minutes. Add the maple syrup and continue cooking until the peaches are caramelized.

To serve, divide the roasted peaches among plates, cut side up. Top with a scoop of vanilla ice cream. Scatter the crumble over top. Drizzle with a touch of Balconville vinegar.

COOK'S NOTE:
You can use other fruits depending on season. Apricots, plums, nectarines, apples, and pears all work well.

SAFWAN THE TATTOO ARTIST

SEAFOOD PLATTER AND MIGNONNETTES
BLOODY CAESAR COCKTAIL SAUCE
LEMON TART

Back when I got my first tattoo, the culture wasn't what it is today. Getting a tattoo was more of a big deal, and for sure it was something rebellious I wanted to do. I wasn't a badass or a biker, I wasn't out to prove anything, but I really liked tattoos and I wanted to get one. In those days the standard-issue tattoos were dragons and daggers with snakes, tribal stuff, tigers. I wanted to do my own thing.

I've always had a fascination with tattoos, even when I was a little kid. When I was around twelve, I told my mom that one day I was going to get one. When she asked me what it would be, I told her skulls with flames—a mother's dream! She said, "No, Charles, stop teasing!" Little did she know, I really wasn't.

When I was around nineteen, I worked at a Montreal bar called Roy Bar, conveniently located next to a tattoo parlour. My buddy Paul was an artist there, so after I was finished my bartending shift one night we decided to go next door and have a couple more drinks. That night, I had these crazy nightmares that I'd gotten a tattoo and I woke up in a cold sweat. When I looked down at my arm, I saw three skulls with flames and the word MOM in the centre. I have to say, it was not amazing. Shortly after, I took my mom out to dinner to break the news. She was not impressed, but at least she knew my heart was in the right place, and she couldn't say I hadn't warned her.

That's when I realized that when you get a tattoo it's with you forever, so you might as well get something you love. Which explains why now I have a big shrimp tattoo, an oyster, a crab, a lobster, clams, fish, and I'm still getting more . . . twenty and counting! I know I'm not the first person to get food tattoos, but my passion for food was something I knew I would always have, so it just made sense.

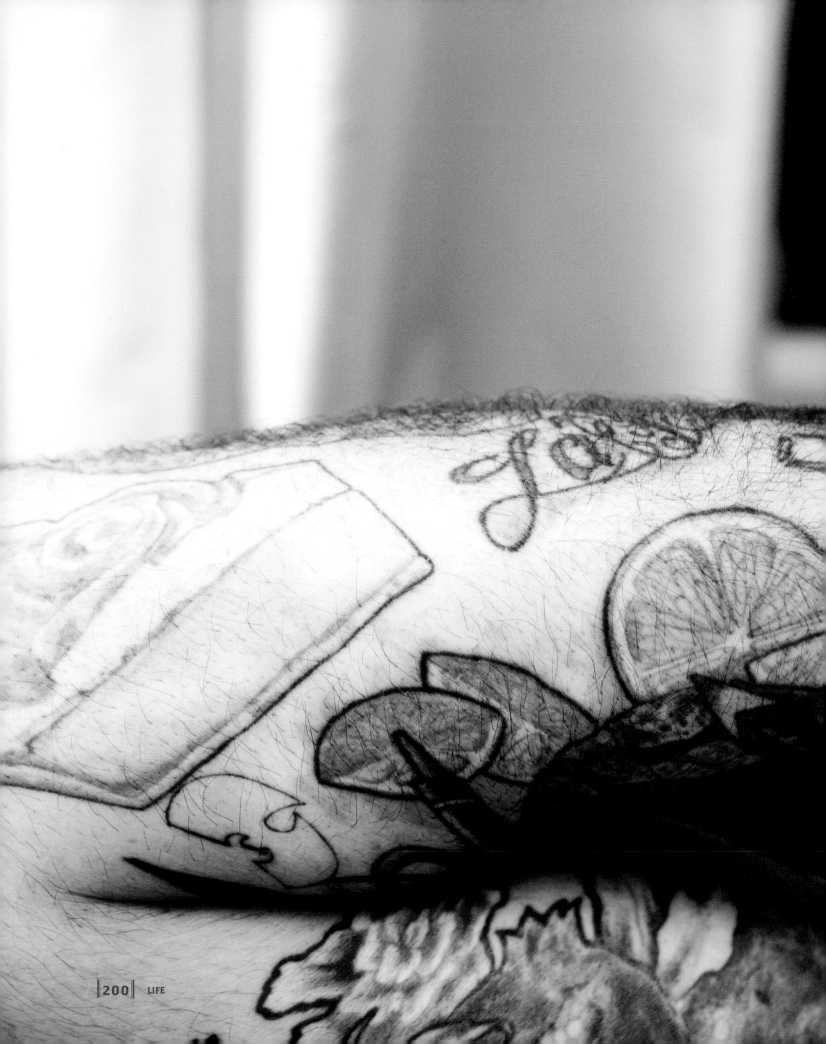

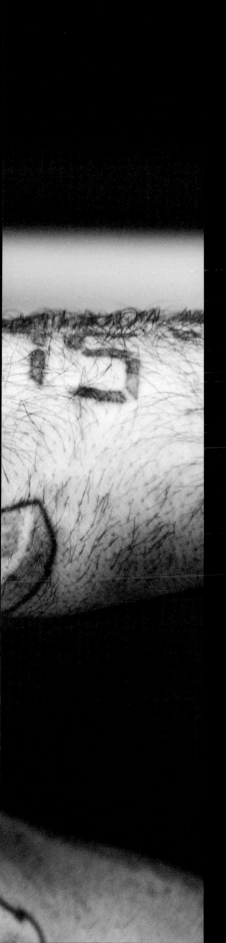

A lot of my tattoos are like souvenirs. I got a durian fruit (the king of fruits) in Singapore, the Virgin of Guadalupe in Mexico, a skull in Guatemala, and a shrimp in Vancouver. My tattoos are not all from positive places and times, though; some of them bring back memories in my life I'd rather not revisit. But all of them remind me of how much my life has changed and reflect who I am.

My tattoos also remind me of people. Safwan is the artist behind some of my favourite tattoos, like my lobster, my oyster, and my mermaid. I met him around the time I got my first tattoo, and we've been friends since. Safwan is a great guy, but more importantly, he's a great friend. And on top of it all, he loves food.

The menu I created for him is my favourite kind of meal—seafood, seafood, and more seafood.

SEAFOOD PLATTER
AND MIGNONNETTES

PREP 30 MIN × SERVES 6 TO 8

The ultimate impressive dish, this seafood platter is perfect for wowing your family and friends. A mignonnette is a vinegar-based sauce that complements the platter. They keep, covered, in the fridge for a month.

SEAFOOD PLATTER

- 12 medium oysters such as Raspberry Point or Malpeque, shucked (page 135), returned to the half shell
- 12 large head-on shrimp, peeled (tail shells left intact), deveined, and poached (page 234)
- 12 scallops on the shell
- 12 fresh raw clams, shucked (in season)
- 4 steamed crab sections, cracked
- 1 whole steamed lobster (about 2 lb/900 g), cracked

GARNISHES

- Lemon wedges
- Hot pepper sauce
- Grated fresh horseradish
- Breads
- Mignonnettes (recipes follow)
- Bloody Caesar Cocktail Sauce (page 204)

Arrange the oysters on a bed of crushed ice; serve with lemon wedges, hot pepper sauce, and grated horseradish.

Arrange the other seafood on a large platter; serve with breads, mignonnettes, and cocktail sauce. Garnish with lemon wedges.

CELERY MIGNONNETTE
PREP 5 MIN × MAKES 1 CUP (250 ML)

- 1/2 celery rib, peeled and finely chopped
- 1/2 shallot, finely chopped
- 1/4 red bell pepper, finely chopped
- 1/4 jalapeño pepper, seeded and finely chopped
- 1/2 cup (125 mL) white wine vinegar
- 1½ teaspoons (7 mL) black peppercorns, crushed
- 1 teaspoon (5 mL) sugar

In a jar, mix all the ingredients.

JALAPEÑO MIGNONNETTE
PREP 5 MIN × MAKES 1 CUP (250 ML)

- Zest and juice of 1/2 orange
- Zest and juice of 1/2 lemon
- Zest and juice of 1/2 lime
- 1 shallot, finely chopped
- 1/2 jalapeño pepper, seeded and finely chopped
- 1/2 cup (125 mL) white balsamic vinegar
- 1 tablespoon (15 mL) black peppercorns, crushed

In a jar, mix all the ingredients.

SAKE MIGNONNETTE
PREP 5 MIN × COOK 5 MIN × MAKES 1 CUP (250 ML)

- 3 tablespoons (45 mL) sake
- 2/3 shallot, finely chopped
- 2/3 green onion, finely chopped
- 2/3 cup (150 mL) rice wine vinegar
- 3 tablespoons (45 mL) orange juice
- 3 tablespoons (45 mL) grapefruit juice
- 1 tablespoon (15 mL) lemon juice
- 2 teaspoons (10 mL) minced fresh ginger
- 2 teaspoons (10 mL) black peppercorns, crushed

In a small saucepan, bring the sake to a boil; simmer for about 5 minutes to remove the alcohol. Let cool.

In a jar, mix all the ingredients.

APPLE MIGNONNETTE
PREP 5 MIN × MAKES 1 CUP (250ML)

- 1/2 McIntosh apple, cored and finely chopped
- 1/2 shallot, finely chopped
- 1/4 cup (60 mL) cider vinegar
- 1/4 cup (60 mL) white balsamic vinegar
- 1½ teaspoons (7 mL) black peppercorns, crushed
- 1 teaspoon (5 mL) brown sugar

In a jar, mix all the ingredients.

BLOODY CAESAR COCKTAIL SAUCE

PREP 15 MIN × COOK 20 MIN × MAKES 2 CUPS (500 mL)

Like the classic Caesar, this seafood dip is brightened with a hit of vodka.

REDUCED CLAM JUICE
- 1 onion, chopped
- 1 garlic clove, chopped
- 1 celery rib, chopped
- 1/2 cup (125 mL) clam juice

COCKTAIL SAUCE
- 1 celery rib, finely chopped
- Zest and juice of 1 lemon
- 1 cup (250 mL) ketchup
- 1/4 cup (60 mL) Worcestershire sauce
- 3 tablespoons (45 mL) vodka
- 2 tablespoons (30 mL) grated fresh horseradish
- 1 tablespoon (15 mL) prepared horseradish
- 1 teaspoon (5 mL) hot pepper sauce
- 1 teaspoon (5 mL) celery seeds
- 1/2 teaspoon (2 mL) chili flakes
- Salt and freshly cracked black pepper

FOR THE REDUCED CLAM JUICE:
In a small saucepan, combine the onion, garlic, celery, and clam juice. Cook on medium heat until reduced by half, about 20 minutes. Strain into a medium bowl, discarding the solids; let cool.

FOR THE COCKTAIL SAUCE:
To the reduced clam juice, add the celery, lemon zest and juice, ketchup, Worcestershire sauce, vodka, fresh horseradish, prepared horseradish, hot pepper sauce, celery seeds, and chili flakes. Season with salt and pepper. Refrigerate until ready to serve.

LEMON TART

PREP 30 MIN PLUS 30 MIN CHILLING × COOK 55 MIN PLUS 1 HOUR FOR DRYING × SERVES 6

I love lemon tart so much, I've even got a tattoo of one on my arm. Now that's dedication! There's just something so light and refreshing about this zesty dessert, and with olive oil crème fraîche in the mix, I just can't get enough.

CANDIED LEMON ZEST
- 2 lemons
- 1/2 cup (125 mL) sugar
- 1/2 cup (125 mL) water

SHORTBREAD PASTRY SHELLS
- 1 cup (250 mL) all-purpose flour
- 1/2 cup (125 mL) icing sugar
- Zest of 1 lemon
- 3/4 cup (175 mL) cold butter, cubed
- 2 large egg yolks

LEMON CURD
- 1/2 cup (125 mL) sugar
- 1/2 cup (125 mL) lemon juice
- 1/2 cup (125 mL) butter, cubed
- 1/4 cup (60 mL) whipping cream
- 2 large eggs
- 2 large egg yolks

OLIVE OIL CRÈME FRAÎCHE
- 1/2 cup (125 mL) crème fraîche
- 2 tablespoons (30 mL) good-quality extra-virgin olive oil
- 1 tablespoon (15 mL) brown sugar

GARNISH
- Fresh blueberries

FOR THE CANDIED LEMON ZEST:
Using a vegetable peeler or small knife, remove long strips of peel from the lemons. Scrape away any white pith. Cut the peel into julienne strips. Place in a small saucepan and cover with cold water. Simmer over medium heat for 7 minutes. Drain. Return the lemon strips to the pan and add the sugar and 1/2 cup (125 mL) water. Simmer over low heat until the zest is translucent and the syrup is slightly thickened, 10 to 15 minutes. Drain.

Transfer the candied lemon zest to a baking sheet lined with parchment paper and set aside to dry for about 1 hour.

FOR THE SHORTBREAD PASTRY SHELLS:
In a food processor, combine the flour, icing sugar, and lemon zest; pulse to mix. Add the butter; process until coarse crumbs form. Add the egg yolks; process just until the dough forms a ball. Flatten the dough into a disc, wrap in plastic wrap, and refrigerate for 30 minutes.

Preheat oven to 325°F (160°C).

Roll out the dough to 1/8-inch (3 mm) thickness. Cut out four 5-inch (12 cm) circles and press dough onto the bottom and up the sides of four 3-inch (8 cm) tartlet pans with removable bottoms. Dough should come up the sides at least 1 inch (2.5 cm). (You can also line an 8- or 9-inch/20- or 23-cm tart pan with removable bottom.)

Prick dough all over with a fork. Chill for 30 minutes. Arrange on a small baking sheet and bake for 8 to 10 minutes, until the pastry looks dry; there should be little to no colour. Cool on a rack. Remove tart shells from the pans and arrange on the baking sheet.

Reduce oven temperature to 275°F (140°C).

FOR THE LEMON CURD:
In the top of a double boiler or in a large heatproof bowl over simmering water, whisk together the sugar, lemon juice, butter, cream, eggs, and egg yolks. Whisk constantly until the mixture is thick enough to coat the back of a spoon, 15 to 20 minutes. Lower the heat if necessary to prevent the eggs from curdling. Strain through a fine-mesh sieve into a clean bowl. Press plastic wrap directly on the surface of the curd and let cool for 10 minutes.

Fill the tart shells with the curd. Bake until the curd is just set, about 10 minutes. Cool on a rack.

FOR THE OLIVE OIL CRÈME FRAÎCHE:
Beat together the crème fraîche, olive oil, and brown sugar until soft peaks form. Refrigerate until ready to serve.

To serve, garnish the lemon tarts with a dollop of crème fraîche, fresh blueberries, and candied lemon zest.

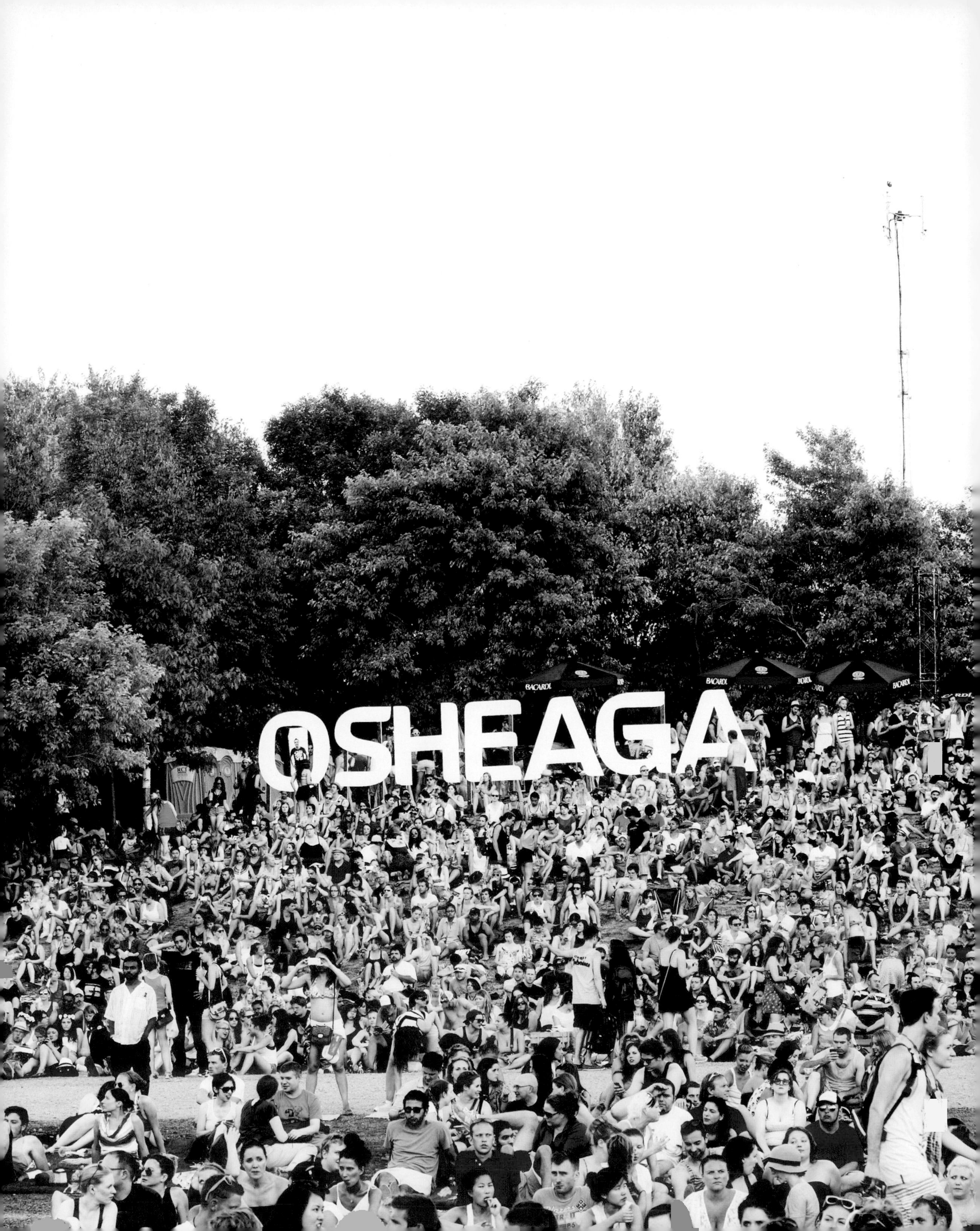
OSHEAGA

THE

CONCERT PROMOTERS

FISH TACOS

HATCH CHILI SAUCE

LOBSTER COBB SALAD

BLACK PEPPER GENERAL TAO'S CHICKEN

Back when I was in cooking school, I had a roommate named Matt who belonged to a now defunct Montreal punk rock band called Men "O" Steel. They used to tour with another band, Reset, who have since evolved into Simple Plan and gone on to become a mega success. I happened to have a big baby-blue GMC van that I would use to help the guys go from gig to gig, so I basically became their roadie. I was also the guy cooking for these musicians when they hung out at our apartment all the time. When Reset were going to shoot their first music video, they came to me and said, "We basically have $300 for food—can you do it?"

I went from that video to catering backstage for any bands who were passing through and knew about my little side business. I never made any money, but it was a lot of fun. Then one summer a local label had a stage at Vans Warped Tour and asked me to do the catering for their artists during the festival. We had shows in Montreal, Toronto, Boston, and Ottawa, and I think the budget was $1000 for food. I never slept—I basically cooked and partied the entire time. I was totally in my element, combining music and food.

I continued catering all through cooking school, usually for family and friends (I did the occasional private party), mostly so I could keep cooking and make a little money on the side. The music gigs, though—man, those were the best!

Over ten years later, I found myself catering again, but this time there was nothing little about it. It was at Montreal's Osheaga music festival, one of the best outdoor live music events in the world, and I was cooking for all the artists and VIPs backstage. I got to cook for Sonic Youth, Arcade Fire, Snoop Dogg, the National, the Black Keys, Eminem, Cypress Hill, ASAP Rocky . . . I got to meet everyone and see everything!

None of my catering jobs had ever been near this scale. I had to make breakfast, lunch, and dinner for about a thousand people every day, over three days. Because Osheaga is so big, I wanted the food to be over the top. Our crew set up a massive outdoor kitchen with everything we needed—deep-fryers, flat grills, ovens, spit grills, even a smoker. Inside a huge white tent we created a market-style fruit stand, a shake bar, a depanneur filled with candy and chocolate bars, an oyster bar, and, the pièce de résistance, an original fairground hot dog machine. It was one of the most challenging jobs I've ever done, but to be a part of all of this, in one of the most beautiful settings—Parc Jean-Drapeau, a little island just outside the city—was incredible. When the sun was out and the heat was blazing, the music was playing, and everyone was having a good time, there was nowhere else I would rather have been.

We made jerk crab, smoked salmon, pulled pork, smoked chicken, tacos, salads, corn on the cob, BBQ shrimp, Montreal smoked meat—it was a total food explosion! I think everyone was pretty blown away when they realized that the combination of amazing food and great music really set this festival apart from all the others on the summer circuit.

One of the promoters who had asked me to cater backstage at Osheaga, Nick, was someone I had met doing the Vans Warped Tour. I was just a kid cooking his ass off back then, probably pretty unremarkable, so it was cool to know that when he asked me to do this festival, he actually remembered me from back in the day. Both Nick and his right-hand man, Dan, are great guys. They know their music and they also know their food.

The following year I catered Osheaga again, but also got to do Heavy MTL, a heavy metal festival in Montreal. I wouldn't have been able to pull it off without the confidence and help of Nick, Dan, the Evenko production team (including my cousins Ben and Rick),

FISH TACOS

PREP 35 MIN × COOK 5 MIN × SERVES 6

These tacos are a personal favourite. The beer batter guarantees extra crunch while the avocado cream and pico de gallo are fresh and flavourful.

AVOCADO CREAM

- 2 avocados, halved, pitted, and cut in chunks
- 1/2 cup (125 mL) thick plain yogurt or sour cream
- Zest and juice of 1 lime
- 1/2 jalapeño pepper, diced
- A few drops of hot green pepper sauce, to taste
- Leaves from 1 bunch of cilantro
- Salt and freshly cracked black pepper

PICO DE GALLO

- 2 tomatoes, seeded and chopped
- 1 onion, finely chopped
- 1 red bell pepper, chopped
- 1 jalapeño pepper, seeded and finely chopped
- 1 garlic clove, minced
- A handful of fresh cilantro leaves
- Zest and juice of 1 lime
- 2 tablespoons (30 mL) olive oil
- Salt and freshly cracked black pepper

BEER BATTER

- 1 cup (250 mL) all-purpose flour
- 1/4 cup (60 mL) cornstarch
- 1 tablespoon (15 mL) baking powder
- Salt
- 2 eggs
- 1½ cups (375 mL) beer

FISH

- Canola oil for deep-frying
- 1 lb (450 g) haddock fillets, cut in large cubes
- All-purpose flour for dusting
- Salt and freshly cracked black pepper

FOR SERVING

- Corn tortillas (page 214)
- Finely shredded iceberg lettuce
- Hatch Chili Sauce (page 215)

FOR THE AVOCADO CREAM:
In a food processor, combine the avocado, yogurt, lime zest and juice, jalapeño, hot pepper sauce, and cilantro; purée until smooth. Season with salt and pepper. Refrigerate until ready to serve.

FOR THE PICO DE GALLO:
In a medium bowl, combine the tomatoes, onion, red pepper, jalapeño, garlic, cilantro, lime zest and juice, and olive oil. Stir well. Season with salt and pepper. Refrigerate until ready to serve.

FOR THE BEER BATTER:
In a large bowl, whisk together the flour, cornstarch, baking powder, and salt to taste. In another bowl, whisk together the eggs and beer, then quickly stir into the flour mixture (don't worry about a few lumps).

FOR THE FISH:
In a deep-fryer or deep, heavy saucepan, heat 2 inches (5 cm) of canola oil to 375°F (190°C).

Dust fish pieces lightly with flour. Dip into the beer batter, then fry until crisp and golden brown, about 1½ minutes, turning once. Drain on paper towels. Season with salt and pepper.

To serve, spread some avocado cream on each tortilla. Top with 3 pieces of fish and some shredded lettuce. Finish with pico de gallo and Hatch Chili Sauce.

CORN TORTILLAS

PREP 10 MIN × COOK 15 MIN × MAKES 12 TORTILLAS

- **2 cups (500 mL) very fine corn flour (masa harina)**
- **1½ cups (375 mL) water**
- **1 teaspoon (5 mL) salt**

Preheat oven to 200°F (100°C).

In a large bowl, combine the corn flour, water, and salt; mix and knead with your hands to form a flexible, soft, and smooth dough.

Pinch off a small piece of dough, roll it into a ball, and use your hands to flatten it into a circle. If large cracks form, add a little more water to the dough and test again.

Pinch off golf-ball-sized pieces of dough; keep them covered with a damp towel while you shape them. Working with one piece of dough at a time, roll into a ball and flatten between your palms. Set the dough circle on a piece of plastic wrap and cover with another piece of plastic wrap. Use a tortilla press or the bottom of a heavy cast-iron pan to flatten the dough into a 6-inch (15 cm) tortilla. Remove the plastic.

Heat a large griddle or large, heavy skillet (preferably cast iron) over medium heat. Cook each tortilla for about 30 seconds on each side or until it looks dry and is brown in spots. Wrap in foil and keep warm in the oven.

HATCH CHILI SAUCE

PREP 15 MIN × COOK 1 HOUR 5 MIN × SERVES 6

Hatch chilies are from New Mexico and have a mild to medium heat that's great for a hot sauce.

- **24 Hatch chilies or other mild or medium-hot green peppers (such as jalapeño, Cubanelle, poblano chilies)**
- **1/4 cup (60 mL) olive oil**
- **Salt and freshly cracked black pepper**
- **1 onion, minced**
- **3 garlic cloves, minced**
- **2 tablespoons (30 mL) white vinegar**
- **1 tablespoon (15 mL) ground coriander**
- **A pinch of sugar**
- **2 cups (500 mL) water**
- **1/4 cup (60 mL) chopped fresh cilantro**

Preheat oven to 450°F (230°C).

Place the chilies on a baking sheet lined with parchment paper. Drizzle with half of the olive oil and season with salt. Roast for about 30 minutes, turning after 15 minutes, until the skin is evenly charred.

Transfer the chilies to a bowl, cover with plastic wrap, and let cool. (This will make peeling the chilies easier.) Peel the chilies, remove the stems and seeds, and chop chilies into chunks.

Heat the remaining olive oil in a medium saucepan over medium heat. Add the onion and cook, stirring occasionally, until fragrant, about 2 minutes. Add the roasted chilies, garlic, vinegar, coriander, and sugar; continue to cook, stirring, for 1 minute. Add the water, lower the heat to medium-low, and cook, stirring occasionally, until almost all the liquid has evaporated, about 30 minutes.

Remove from heat. Stir in the cilantro. Season with salt and pepper. Let cool.

LOBSTER COBB SALAD

PREP 20 MIN × SERVES 6 TO 8

I'm from the school of thought that says lobster can be added to pretty much any dish. Here it takes a famous salad to a new level of greatness.

LOBSTER COBB SALAD

- 1 head iceberg lettuce, cut in wedges
- 6 hard-boiled eggs, peeled and sliced
- 8 slices bacon, cooked until crisp, crumbled
- 2 cups (500 mL) watercress
- 2 avocados, halved, pitted, and cubed
- 2 tomatoes, cubed
- Meat from 2 steamed lobsters
- Salt and freshly cracked black pepper
- 1 cup (250 mL) crumbled blue cheese

DRESSING

- 1 tablespoon (15 mL) red wine vinegar
- 1 tablespoon (15 mL) Worcestershire sauce
- 1 tablespoon (15 mL) Dijon mustard
- 1 tablespoon (15 mL) maple syrup
- 1 garlic clove, minced
- Salt and freshly cracked black pepper
- 2 hard-boiled egg yolks
- 1/2 cup (125 mL) olive oil
- About 2 tablespoons (30 mL) finely chopped fresh chives

FOR THE LOBSTER COBB SALAD:

Make a bed of lettuce on a platter, in a shallow serving bowl, or on individual plates. Arrange over the lettuce, in rows or in a checkerboard pattern, the eggs, bacon, watercress, avocados, tomatoes, and lobster meat, covering the lettuce almost completely. Season with salt and pepper.

FOR THE DRESSING:

In a small bowl, whisk together the vinegar, Worcestershire sauce, mustard, maple syrup, garlic, and salt and pepper to taste. Using a fork, mash in the egg yolks to make a paste. While whisking, slowly drizzle in the olive oil to form a thick dressing. Stir in the chives.

To serve, pour some of the dressing over the salad. Sprinkle with the blue cheese. Serve the remaining dressing on the side.

BLACK PEPPER GENERAL TAO'S CHICKEN

PREP 20 MIN PLUS 12 HOURS FOR MARINATING × COOK 35 MIN × SERVES 6

If you like heat, you're going to love this recipe inspired by a dish I had in Singapore. Here's a little trick—the spicier you want it, the finer you crush the peppercorns.

CHICKEN MARINADE
- 1 cup (250 mL) milk
- 1 cup (250 mL) soy sauce
- 2 tablespoons (30 mL) minced fresh ginger
- 1 garlic clove, minced
- 1 lemongrass stalk, chopped
- 1½ lb (675 g) boneless, skinless chicken thighs, cut in cubes

BLACK PEPPER SAUCE
- 2 cups (500 mL) veal stock
- 1/2 cup (125 mL) oyster sauce
- 1/2 cup (125 mL) hoisin sauce
- 1/4 cup (60 mL) orange juice
- 1/4 cup (60 mL) black peppercorns, crushed
- 2 tablespoons (30 mL) minced fresh ginger
- 2 tablespoons (30 mL) soy sauce
- 2 tablespoons (30 mL) mirin
- 2 tablespoons (30 mL) tamarind paste
- 1 garlic clove, minced

DEEP-FRYING THE CHICKEN
- Canola oil for deep-frying
- 1 cup (250 mL) all-purpose flour
- Salt and freshly cracked black pepper

GARNISH
- 4 green onions, finely chopped

FOR THE CHICKEN MARINADE:
In a large bowl, stir together the milk, soy sauce, ginger, garlic, and lemongrass. Add the chicken, turning to coat. Marinate, covered and refrigerated, for at least 12 hours.

FOR THE SAUCE:
In a large skillet, combine the stock, oyster sauce, hoisin sauce, orange juice, peppercorns, ginger, soy sauce, mirin, tamarind paste, and garlic. Simmer for 30 minutes or until syrupy. Set aside and keep warm.

TO DEEP-FRY AND FINISH THE CHICKEN:
In a deep-fryer or deep, heavy saucepan, heat 2 inches (5 cm) of canola oil to 350°F (180°C).

In a bowl, season the flour with salt and pepper. Drain the chicken, discarding the marinade. Dredge the chicken pieces in the flour, shaking off any excess flour. Fry the chicken until golden brown on both sides and cooked through, about 5 minutes.

Meanwhile, reheat the sauce over medium heat. Transfer the fried chicken to the sauce; cook, turning, until the chicken is evenly coated with the sauce.

To serve, transfer the chicken to a platter and garnish with green onions.

THE
DOG WALKERS

Soft-Boiled Egg on Creamy Polenta with Kale and Crispy Serrano Ham

Cheesy Mushroom Melt

The Simplest Chocolate Chip Cookies with Maldon Salt

I'm going to let you in on a little secret: my dog is a vegetarian. I know, I know, it's embarrassing and it goes against everything I believe in, but I can't help it—she loves vegetables, and if that's how she wants to live her life, I'm not going to stop her. Her favourite snack is carrots, and it's at the point where you can't even say the word in front of her because she goes straight for the fridge. My girlfriend, Sabrina, and I have to spell it out if she's around. If not, watch out: as soon as you say the c-word you better have a carrot close at hand or you're going to have to deal with some serious sad puppy eyes.

Maybe I should start at the beginning. Thirteen years ago, I had just finished school, my apartment was over a bar, I was working as a band roadie and doing my catering gig on the side. It was the summer to end all summers—fun work, few responsibilities, and good times all around. Then one day a friend of mine asked if I could drive her to an animal shelter outside of the city so that she could get a dog. Apparently this place in Repentigny was the last stop for animals that hadn't been adopted at the SPCA.

When we got to the shelter and started wandering around, I spotted this puppy staring at me. She was a little rabbit-sized mutt with big paws and the dumbest face I had ever seen. Obviously she saw something she liked because she wouldn't take her eyes off me. Then my friend wanted to leave; she hadn't seen anything she liked. A little angry that we had come all this way for nothing, I got in the car and started driving away. But I couldn't get that dog out of my head. I slammed on the brakes, turned the car around, and headed back to the shelter. I could not leave without that puppy.

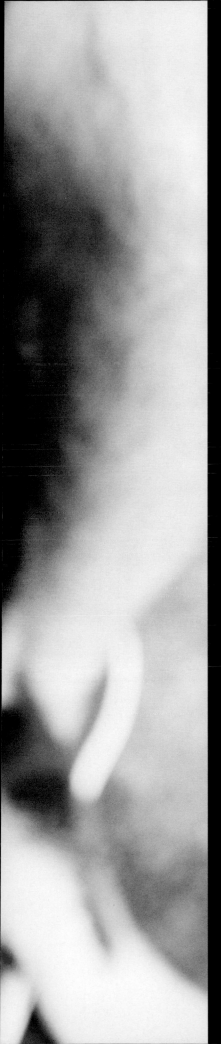

I had never planned to own a dog. I was a dog lover, sure, but I was also twenty-one years old and having a great time. I could barely take care of myself, so how was I supposed to take care of an animal? But I swear to god, as soon as they let her out of that cage she ran up to me, started licking my face, jumping all over me with those big paws, and that was it, I was in love.

She was a cute, fluffy little thing with a funny face, and even though my parents weren't exactly thrilled that I had just adopted a dog, as soon as they saw her she was instantly part of the family. Half Rottweiler, half German shepherd, her official name is Fakey, a skateboarding move, but no one calls her that. We've always called her Filou, which is kind of weird for the people in my family because it's also my cousin's nickname. It's definitely no disrespect to him, but it does cause some confusion at family gatherings.

When Filou and I moved down to Old Montreal many years later, I would often see these two girls walking down the street surrounded by about fifteen dogs on leashes. It was the craziest sight! Given my long hours, I figured hiring these girls might be a good idea for me and Filou. Not only did they walk the pooches, but they were practically dog whisperers. They trained them, groomed them, did dog shows, the whole package.

But despite Marie France and Romy's talents, Filou just didn't take to it. There's a time in your dog's life where you realize there's no point pushing them—you want them to live out the rest of their life happy and comfortable. Filou just wasn't interested in the other dogs, let alone walking with all of them. She was at an age where she needed to chill and do her own thing, and I respected that.

Even though the dog walkers weren't Filou's idea of a good time, I got to know these girls and became friends with them. Filou and I see them all the time on our walks, and they always give her a special little carrot treat.

At this point, Filou's been with me through thick and thin, and when I'm not at work, she's constantly by my side. I chose this dog first and foremost to save her life, but more than that I think she's the one who chose me.

SOFT-BOILED EGG ON CREAMY POLENTA WITH KALE AND CRISPY SERRANO HAM

PREP 30 MIN × COOK 30 MIN × SERVES 4

This is a beautiful recipe to serve at brunch. The perfectly cooked egg, creamy polenta, and sliver of crispy ham create a deliciously sophisticated dish.

SERRANO HAM
- 8 slices Serrano ham

CREAMY POLENTA
- 2 cups (500 mL) chicken stock
- 2 cups (500 mL) milk
- 3 sprigs of cilantro
- 2 garlic cloves
- 1 cup (250 mL) cornmeal
- 1 cup (250 mL) shredded Asiago cheese, plus more for garnish
- Salt and freshly cracked black pepper

KALE
- 2 bunches kale, stems and tough centre ribs discarded
- 1 tablespoon (15 mL) butter
- Juice of 1 lemon
- Salt and freshly cracked black pepper

EGGS
- 4 eggs

FOR THE SERRANO HAM:
Preheat oven to 350°F (180°C).

Arrange the Serrano ham on a baking sheet lined with parchment paper. Cover with another sheet of parchment paper and place another baking sheet on top. (This will keep the ham flat while it cooks.) Bake for 30 minutes or until crispy. Set aside on paper towels.

FOR THE CREAMY POLENTA:
In a large, heavy saucepan, combine the stock, milk, cilantro, and garlic. Bring to a boil, reduce heat to medium, and simmer for 2 minutes to flavour the liquid. Discard the cilantro and garlic. Whisking constantly, add the cornmeal in a steady stream; whisk to remove any lumps. Cook over low heat, stirring often with a wooden spoon, until the polenta is soft, 10 to 15 minutes. Fold in the Asiago cheese. Season. Set aside and keep warm.

FOR THE KALE:
In a large saucepan of boiling water, blanch the kale for 1 minute. Drain and transfer to a bowl of ice water to stop the cooking. Drain again. Using your hands, press out excess water. Chop the kale in half.

In the same saucepan over medium heat, melt the butter. Add the kale and lemon juice; cook for 1 minute. Season with salt and pepper. Set aside and keep warm.

FOR THE EGGS:
Bring a large saucepan of water to a boil. Drop in the eggs and boil for 6 minutes. Using a slotted spoon, transfer the eggs to a bowl and run cold water over them to stop the cooking.

To serve, drain the eggs, rattle them around in the bowl to crack the shells, and carefully peel them. Place a large spoonful of polenta on each plate. Top with the kale and then a soft-boiled egg. Sprinkle with Asiago cheese and garnish each serving with 2 slices of Serrano ham.

COOK'S NOTE:
The polenta can be made ahead and reheated: stir in 1/4 to 1/2 cup (60 to 125 mL) water or stock, cover the pan, and reheat over low heat. (Or reheat in a microwave-safe dish.) Whisk well before serving.

CHEESY MUSHROOM MELT

PREP 20 MIN × COOK 20 MIN × SERVES 4

Upgrade your standard grilled cheese with mushrooms and onions. Replacing that slice of Cheddar with cheesy Mornay sauce takes this staple to new heights.

MUSHROOMS

- 1 tablespoon (15 mL) olive oil
- 10 cipollini onions, peeled and quartered
- 1 lb (450 g) mixed mushrooms, sliced
- 1 garlic clove, minced
- 1 cup (250 mL) veal stock
- Leaves from a small bunch of parsley, chopped
- Salt and freshly cracked black pepper

MORNAY SAUCE

- 2 tablespoons (30 mL) butter
- 2 tablespoons (30 mL) all-purpose flour
- 1 cup (250 mL) milk
- 1 cup (250 mL) shredded Gruyère cheese, plus more for garnish
- Salt and freshly cracked black pepper

CHEESY MUSHROOM MELT

- 2 tablespoons (30 mL) butter, softened
- 8 slices bread

FOR THE MUSHROOMS:

Heat the oil in a large saucepan over medium-high heat. Add the onions and mushrooms; cook, stirring frequently, for 5 minutes or until golden. Add the garlic and continue cooking for 1 minute. Add the veal stock. Simmer for another 5 minutes or until the liquid has reduced. Remove from heat and stir in the parsley. Season with salt and pepper.

FOR THE MORNAY SAUCE:

While the mushrooms are cooking, in a medium saucepan, melt the butter over medium heat. Stir in the flour with a wooden spoon. Cook, stirring, for 2 minutes. Whisk in the milk. Continue cooking, stirring frequently, until the sauce thickens, about 2 minutes. Reduce heat to medium-low. Add the Gruyère; stir until the cheese is completely melted and the sauce is smooth. Remove from heat and season with salt and pepper.

FOR THE CHEESY MUSHROOM MELT:

Heat a large skillet over medium heat.

Butter each slice of bread on one side. Turn over half the slices. Spoon most of the mushroom mixture onto the unbuttered sides; top with the Mornay sauce. Cover with the remaining bread, buttered side up. Cook the sandwiches until golden, about 5 minutes on each side.

To serve, cut the sandwiches in half diagonally; transfer to plates. Top with a spoonful of the remaining mushroom mixture. Garnish with shredded cheese.

THE SIMPLEST CHOCOLATE CHIP COOKIES WITH MALDON SALT

PREP 15 MIN × COOK 18 MIN × MAKES ABOUT 20 COOKIES

No one would guess that the secret to a perfect chocolate chip cookie is salt, but a little sprinkling on top will make you rethink cooking with chocolate forever. It's no wonder when I start eating these, I can't stop.

- 2 cups (500 mL) all-purpose flour
- 1/2 teaspoon (2 mL) baking powder
- 1/2 teaspoon (2 mL) baking soda
- 1 cup (250 mL) butter, softened
- 1¼ cups (310 mL) brown sugar
- 1 large egg
- 1 teaspoon (5 mL) vanilla extract
- 2 cups (500 mL) chopped bittersweet chocolate
- Maldon sea salt

Preheat oven to 350°F (180°C). Line a baking sheet with parchment paper.

Sift the flour, baking powder, and baking soda into a bowl. In a large bowl with an electric mixer, cream the butter with the sugar until very light, about 5 minutes. Beat in the egg and vanilla. Add the flour mixture; mix on low speed just until combined. Stir in the chopped chocolate.

Using a large ice cream scoop, scoop 6 to 8 golf-ball-sized balls of dough onto the baking sheet, about 2 inches (5 cm) apart. Sprinkle lightly with Maldon salt. Bake until golden brown but still soft, 18 to 20 minutes. Repeat with remaining dough. Enjoy warm.

COOK'S NOTE:
The dough can be frozen, wrapped tightly in plastic and foil, for up to 3 months.

THE HOCKEY TEAM

Cocktail Shrimp
Fried Chicken
Creamed Cucumbers
Cheddar Biscuits
Flavoured Butters for Corn on the Cob
Chocolate Pots de Crème

I love hockey. I love talking about it, I love watching it, and more than anything, I love playing it. I'm not exactly the world's most gifted player, but luckily I know a thing or two about food. I'm pretty sure that's the reason I've been asked to join so many local leagues. You'd never think that in a locker room with twenty guys the hot topic would be ways to cook a chicken, or where to get duck prosciutto, but it often is. It's always a plus to own a restaurant when you're in this "beer league" system of people who play hockey for fun. I'm the go-to guy for food questions, tips, and of course reservations. And on a good night I might even score a goal or two.

Hockey is one of those things that I always make time for. It's basically my yoga: it clears my head and lets me step away from my hectic life and focus on something other than work. While I'm on the ice I'm not thinking about anything else—there's no cell phones or music, no orders coming in or pots and pans on the stove, just a bunch of people playing for the love of the game. None of us made it to the big show, but when someone scores a goal it's as though we just won the Stanley Cup, and out of everyone I'm probably cheering the loudest. It's actually a bit embarrassing, but I can't wipe the smile off my face.

When I was a kid, at Christmastime my cousins and I would play hockey all day while the adults got dinner ready. We'd come in as the sun was going down, scoff down our meals, and then pass out in total food comas. The next morning, we'd get up and do it all over again. Best holidays ever.

Working in the restaurant industry for so long, and Montreal being the hockey city it is, I've had the chance to meet and cook for generations of NHL players. As you can imagine, I get pretty star-struck.

I mean, these guys are my heroes! I totally respect them because they're so good at what they do. And I've come to realize that they also like what I'm doing here. It's wild, but these guys who I watch on TV all winter keep on coming back for my food! I would never in a million years have imagined that my hockey idols would be enjoying meals in my restaurant . . . and man, do they have an appetite!

Beyond having fun on the ice, playing hockey allows me to become friends with people I otherwise wouldn't get a chance to meet. The players on my teams are from all walks of life. They are doctors and lawyers, writers, contractors, stay-at-home dads, and semi-employed hipsters. All you have to do is love the game and you're in—although it helps if you know how to skate!

Playing hockey is a lot like working in a restaurant. Seriously! Both are physically demanding activities where the collective drive is to play the best we can together no matter what. When I gather my staff and give them that pep talk before a busy night, we have a plan about how things are going to work and everyone is in position, ready to go. It's a lot like being out on the ice, ready for a game. It's about giving it your all, right until the end.

I think anyone who's ever laced up skates would agree: hockey is a great way to let off some steam, get that heart rate going, and have a good time. Whether it's in pickup leagues with my friends now, or practising on an outdoor rink in forty-below weather with my kids in the future, I always want hockey to be a part of my life.

COCKTAIL SHRIMP

PREP 15 MIN × COOK 1½ MIN × SERVES 6

The key to this simple recipe is to poach the shrimp before you peel them so that they keep their shape.

- 1 onion, chopped
- 1 head of garlic, halved crosswise
- 2 celery ribs, coarsely chopped
- 1 bottle (2 oz/57 mL) hot pepper sauce
- 1/4 cup (60 mL) salt
- 24 large tiger shrimp (not peeled)
- Salt and freshly cracked black pepper
- Bloody Caesar Cocktail Sauce (page 204)

Bring a large saucepan of water to a boil. Add the onion, garlic, celery, hot pepper sauce, and salt. Add the shrimp and cook for 1½ minutes.

Drain the shrimp and transfer to a bowl of ice water to stop the cooking. Drain again. Peel, keeping the tail shells intact, and devein. Refrigerate until ready to serve. Serve with Bloody Caesar Cocktail Sauce.

FRIED CHICKEN

PREP 15 MIN PLUS 6 HOURS FOR MARINATING × COOK 15 MIN × SERVES 4

This recipe is always a crowd pleaser. To get that perfect outer crunch, I suggest investing in a deep-fryer. You don't have to break the bank, and having one in your kitchen arsenal makes all the difference.

- **1 whole chicken, cut in 8 pieces**
- **Canola oil for deep-frying**
- **1 egg**

BUTTERMILK MARINADE
- **3 cups (750 mL) buttermilk**
- **4 garlic cloves, smashed**
- **4 sprigs of thyme**

SEASONED FLOUR
- **2 cups (500 mL) all-purpose flour**
- **1 tablespoon (15 mL) onion powder**
- **1 tablespoon (15 mL) garlic powder**
- **1 tablespoon (15 mL) paprika**
- **1 tablespoon (15 mL) dry mustard**
- **1½ teaspoons (7 mL) salt**
- **1 teaspoon (5 mL) cracked black pepper**
- **1/2 teaspoon (2 mL) baking powder**

FOR THE BUTTERMILK MARINADE:
In a large bowl, combine the buttermilk, garlic, and thyme. Add the chicken pieces, turning to coat. Cover and refrigerate for at least 6 hours or overnight.

FOR THE SEASONED FLOUR:
In a large bowl, whisk together all the ingredients.

FOR DEEP-FRYING THE CHICKEN:
In a deep-fryer or deep, heavy saucepan, heat 3 inches (8 cm) of canola oil to 325°F (160°C).

Drain the chicken, reserving the marinade. Discard the garlic and thyme. Whisk the egg into the marinade.

Working in batches, toss the chicken pieces in the seasoned flour. Dip in the marinade, then in the flour again. Set aside on a plate. Working in batches, fry the chicken, turning occasionally, for about 12 minutes or until golden brown and crispy and a thermometer inserted in the centre of a drumstick reads 180°F (82°C). Drain on paper towels.

Serve with Creamed Cucumbers (page 238), corn on the cob with flavoured butters (page 239), and Cheddar Biscuits (page 238).

CREAMED CUCUMBERS

PREP 5 MIN × SERVES 4

Although this recipe looks really basic, it was my grandfather Jean-Claude's favourite and always has people going back for seconds.

- 2 English cucumbers, peeled in alternating strips, cubed
- 1/2 cup (125 mL) whipping cream
- Salt and freshly cracked black pepper

In a bowl, stir together the cucumbers and cream. Season with salt and pepper. Refrigerate until ready to serve.

CHEDDAR BISCUITS

PREP 15 MIN × COOK 15 MIN × MAKES ABOUT 12 BISCUITS

Nothing goes better with fried chicken than some good old-fashioned biscuits. Buttery and flaky, these ones will become a household favourite, guaranteed.

- 3½ cups (875 mL) all-purpose flour
- 2 tablespoons (30 mL) baking powder
- 1 tablespoon (15 mL) sugar
- 2 teaspoons (10 mL) cayenne pepper
- Salt and freshly cracked black pepper
- 2/3 cup (150 mL) cold butter, cubed
- 2 cups (500 mL) shredded sharp Cheddar cheese
- 1¾ cups (425 mL) buttermilk
- 1/4 cup (60 mL) butter, melted

Preheat oven to 450°F (230°C). Line a baking sheet with parchment paper.

In a large bowl, whisk together the flour, baking powder, sugar, cayenne, and salt and black pepper to taste.

Using a pastry blender, two knives, or your fingers, cut in the butter until the mixture resembles coarse cornmeal. Stir in the cheese. Add the buttermilk and stir just until combined. Do not overmix or your biscuits will be tough.

Turn the dough out onto a lightly floured work surface. Using your hands or a rolling pin, flatten the dough to about 1/2-inch (1 cm) thickness. Using a 3-inch (8 cm) round cutter, cut out biscuits. Gently press scraps together and cut out more biscuits. Arrange on the baking sheet.

Bake for 15 minutes or until nicely browned. Brush the biscuits with melted butter. Serve warm.

FLAVOURED BUTTERS FOR CORN ON THE COB

PREP 15 MIN PLUS 30 MINUTES FOR CHILLING × SERVES 8

Corn on the cob is a summer staple, but sometimes it's nice to dress up an old favourite in something new. You can serve the corn with one, two, or all three flavoured butters.

JALAPEÑO AND LIME BUTTER

- 1 cup (250 mL) butter, softened
- 2 jalapeño peppers, roasted, peeled, seeded, and chopped
- Zest and juice of 1 lime
- 2 tablespoons (30 mL) finely chopped fresh chives
- 1 tablespoon (15 mL) honey
- Salt and freshly cracked black pepper

ROASTED GARLIC BUTTER

- 1 cup (250 mL) butter, softened
- 1 head of roasted garlic (page 150)
- 2 tablespoons (30 mL) chopped fresh parsley
- Salt and freshly cracked black pepper

TOGARASHI AND MAPLE BUTTER

- 1 cup (250 mL) butter, softened
- 1 tablespoon (15 mL) shichimi togarashi (Japanese seven-spice blend)
- 1 tablespoon (15 mL) maple syrup
- Salt and freshly cracked black pepper

TO MAKE EACH BUTTER:

In a bowl, mash the butter with a spatula. Stir in the remaining ingredients.

Scrape the flavoured butter onto a sheet of wax paper. Shape the butter into a log and roll up in the paper. Refrigerate for at least 30 minutes or up to 3 days. (*The butter may also be frozen. Thaw in the fridge before using.*)

Serve with corn on the cob.

CHOCOLATE POTS DE CRÈME

PREP 10 MIN PLUS 8 HOURS FOR CHILLING × COOK 35 MIN × SERVES 6

This dessert is all about luscious, creamy texture. Try to use a good quality chocolate to really satisfy that sweet tooth.

CHOCOLATE POTS DE CRÈME

- 12 oz (340 g) good-quality bittersweet chocolate, chopped (2 cups/500 mL)
- 1 cup (250 mL) whipping cream
- 1 cup (250 mL) whole milk
- 6 large egg yolks
- 1/4 cup (60 mL) sugar

WHIPPED COFFEE CREAM

- 1 cup (250 mL) whipping cream
- 2 tablespoons (30 mL) icing sugar
- 2 tablespoons (30 mL) brewed espresso or strong coffee

FOR THE POTS DE CRÈME:
Position a rack in the centre of the oven and preheat oven to 325°F (160°C). Put six 1/2-cup (125 mL) ramekins or heatproof cups in a large roasting pan or baking dish with high sides.

Place the chopped chocolate in a medium bowl. In a saucepan, warm the cream and milk together. In another medium bowl, vigorously whisk the egg yolks with the sugar for 1 minute. Stirring constantly, slowly add about half of the warm cream mixture. Pour the egg mixture back into the saucepan. Cook over low heat, stirring constantly, until the custard thickens enough to coat the back of a spoon, about 3 minutes. Pour over the chopped chocolate. Let sit for 5 minutes, then slowly whisk until smooth and creamy.

Divide the custard among the ramekins. Pour enough boiling water into the pan to come halfway up the sides of the ramekins.

Cover the pan tightly with foil. Bake custards for 30 minutes or until set around the edges but still slightly jiggly in the centre; an instant-read thermometer inserted in the centre should register 150 to 155°F (65 to 68°C). Uncover the custards and let cool to room temperature in the water bath.

Remove the custards from the bath, cover them with plastic wrap, and refrigerate for at least 8 hours.

FOR THE WHIPPED COFFEE CREAM:
In a large bowl, beat the cream with the sugar and espresso until soft peaks form. Refrigerate until ready to use.

To serve, garnish the chocolate pots de crème with whipped coffee cream.

ALEX THE TRAINER

HERB AND FRESH CHICKPEA SALAD WITH TOASTED PITA CHIPS
CEVICHE
GREEN PAELLA
STEAMED CARROT CAKE WITH HONEY YOGURT FROSTING

My job means that I'm eating all the time. I'm constantly trying this and tasting that—there's no escaping it. It's the slow grazing and the tasting of each dish that can add up in this industry. You eat a couple of fries on the fly, grab a piece of bacon here, a little bit of cheese there. All of a sudden you have no idea how much you've eaten and you're hanging out with your new best friends: fat ass and muffin top.

Eating healthy, balanced meals and working out every day is definitely the way to go for me. Recently, I've started taking responsibility for what I put in my body, which means watching portion size, eating lots of fresh fruits and vegetables, and as much as possible, making fitness part of a daily routine.

I work out every day and I honestly feel on top of the world. There's nothing better than being comfortable in your own skin. It's got nothing to do with being ripped or being rake thin. It's all about feeling good and feeling good about yourself. And of course, cheating. Because c'mon, if you can't let yourself indulge once in a while, what's the point?

My cheat day is usually Saturday, and I go for the usual culprits: burgers, fries, pizza, fried chicken, and hot dogs. Occasionally I'll indulge in a sushi orgy, which sounds healthy until you see how much of it I eat. No matter what, my cheat day is always topped off with a batch of Maldon salt chocolate chip cookies fresh from the oven. The next day, it's back to steamed fish and veggies!

I've always been a pretty active guy, but I only started training and going to the gym regularly about five years ago. My buddy Alex, who used to be a manager at Garde Manger and is now a full-time personal

trainer, encouraged me to train with him. Trying to keep up with him was a challenge at first. It's good to have a guy who's a little faster, stronger, and in better shape to work out with—it pushes you all the more. Alex not only instilled in me a drive for health and fitness but helped create a workout crew among the restaurant staff. I sincerely believe that having a healthy lifestyle is reflected in the restaurant's performance as a whole.

In the restaurant industry, it's hard not to get caught up in the late nights, the drinking, the eating, and the overindulgence. Just as in any job, there are always excuses to eat badly and not be active. It's all about finding the balance that works for you and sticking to it. I was lucky to be influenced by someone like Alex who opened my eyes to the idea that taking care of my body could make all the difference. It's about getting out there, taking that first step, and sweating it out. Oh, and cheating—that's the part that makes it all worthwhile. Whether it's a piece of chocolate cake or a meal at your favourite restaurant, it's important to enjoy the simple pleasures of food.

HERB AND FRESH CHICKPEA SALAD WITH TOASTED PITA CHIPS

PREP 30 MIN PLUS 1 HOUR FOR SOAKING × COOK 10 MIN × SERVES 8

Fresh chickpeas really make this dish a standout, but canned or cooked dried ones will do the trick in a pinch. I use sumac in this recipe, a Middle Eastern spice that's a bit new for me. It adds a lemony zing to this fresh and healthy salad.

TOASTED PITA CHIPS

- 1 pita bread
- 1 garlic clove, crushed and peeled
- 1 tablespoon (15 mL) olive oil
- Coarse salt and freshly cracked black pepper

FRESH CHICKPEA SALAD

- 3 cups (750 mL) water
- 1/2 cup (125 mL) salt
- 2 cups (500 mL) fresh chickpeas (garbanzo beans), shelled
- About 12 grape tomatoes, halved
- 1/2 English cucumber, peeled, seeded, and cut in 1/2-inch (1 cm) chunks
- 1/2 red onion, thinly sliced
- 1 cup (250 mL) fresh peas, blanched (in season)
- 1/4 cup (60 mL) olive oil
- Zest and juice of 1 lemon
- 2 good handfuls of fresh parsley leaves, chopped
- Leaves from 1 sprig of oregano
- 1/2 cup (125 mL) fresh mint leaves
- 1/2 cup (125 mL) celery leaves
- 1/2 teaspoon (2 mL) ground sumac
- Maldon sea salt and freshly cracked black pepper

FOR THE PITA CHIPS:

Preheat oven to 400°F (200°C).

Split the pita to create two circles. Rub with garlic and drizzle with olive oil. Season with salt and pepper. Bake on a baking sheet for 10 minutes or until golden brown and crisp. Set aside.

FOR THE CHICKPEA SALAD:

In a bowl, combine the water and salt; stir to dissolve the salt. Add the chickpeas. Let soak for 1 hour. Drain and rinse the chickpeas.

In a large bowl, combine the chickpeas, tomatoes, cucumber, onion, and peas. Add the olive oil, lemon zest, and lemon juice. Toss to coat evenly. Add the parsley, oregano, mint, celery, and sumac. Season with Maldon salt and pepper. Toss again. Crunch the toasted pita bread in your hands to make smaller pieces and scatter them over the salad.

CEVICHE

PREP 5 MIN PLUS 1 HOUR FOR MARINATING × SERVES 4

I use hot amarillo chilies from Peru in this bright, zesty ceviche. If you can't find them fresh, you can usually get them dried at specialty shops, or substitute a habanero or other hot chili. For a further twist, I've added white shoyu, a less salty, more tangy Japanese white soy sauce. Whenever you make ceviche, use the freshest seafood you can find.

CEVICHE

- 1 fresh ají amarillo, seeded and minced
- 1 small garlic clove, minced
- 1 shallot, thinly sliced
- Zest and juice of 2 limes
- Zest and juice of 2 lemons
- 3 tablespoons (45 mL) extra-virgin olive oil
- Salt and freshly cracked black pepper
- 4 large scallops, sliced horizontally
- 1/2 lb (225 g) firm white-fleshed fish fillets, such as New Brunswick sturgeon or farmed striped bass, cubed
- 1/2 lb (225 g) fresh shrimp from Florida or BC spot prawns, peeled and deveined

GARNISHES

- Dash of white shoyu (white soy sauce)
- Grapefruit segments
- Micro cilantro leaves
- Micro arugula
- Maldon sea salt and freshly cracked black pepper

FOR THE CEVICHE:

In a large bowl, stir together the ají amarillo, garlic, shallot, lime zest and juice, lemon zest and juice, and olive oil. Season with salt and pepper. Add the scallops, fish, and shrimp; gently toss with the marinade. Marinate, covered and refrigerated, for about 1 hour before serving.

To serve, divide the ceviche among plates or bowls. Add a touch of shoyu and garnish with grapefruit and micro greens. Sprinkle with Maldon salt and pepper.

COOK'S NOTE:

White shoyu is clearer and thinner than traditional dark soy sauce. It has a light amber colour that doesn't darken foods. With a remarkable flavour that elevates foods without overwhelming them, it's an ideal accompaniment to sushi and sashimi, seafood, clear soups, tofu, and steamed vegetables. It also makes a great marinade when blended with olive oil. It can be found in most Asian grocery stores or specialty food stores.

GREEN PAELLA

PREP 30 MIN × COOK 25 MIN × SERVES 6

This is my take on paella. Instead of using saffron, I use a cilantro paste similar to pesto. Not only does it make the dish an incredible green but it tastes light, bright, and delicious.

CILANTRO PASTE

- 2 poblano chilies, roasted, peeled, and seeded
- 1/2 cup (125 mL) cilantro leaves and stems
- 1/2 cup (125 mL) coarsely chopped saltwort
- 1 garlic clove, chopped
- 1 shallot, chopped
- Zest and juice of 1 lime
- 1/4 cup (60 mL) extra-virgin olive oil
- 1 tablespoon (15 mL) sugar
- 1/2 teaspoon (2 mL) coriander seeds, crushed
- A pinch of cayenne pepper
- Kosher salt and freshly cracked black pepper

PAELLA

- 1/4 cup (60 mL) extra-virgin olive oil
- 1 onion, chopped
- 4 garlic cloves, chopped
- 1/2 lb (225 g) boneless, skinless chicken thighs
- 1/4 lb (112 g) cured chorizo, sliced
- 3 cups (750 mL) Bomba rice or other short-grain rice such as arborio
- 6 cups (1.5 L) hot chicken or veal stock
- 1 lb (450 g) clams, scrubbed
- 1 lb (450 g) mussels, scrubbed
- 1 lb (450 g) baby kale leaves, blanched and drained
- Salt and freshly cracked black pepper
- 6 large scallops
- 8 large shrimp, peeled and deveined
- 4 green onions, finely chopped

FOR THE CILANTRO PASTE:

In a food processor, combine the poblano chilies, cilantro, saltwort, garlic, shallot, lime zest and juice, olive oil, sugar, coriander, and cayenne. Pulse until a coarse purée forms. Season with salt and pepper.

FOR THE PAELLA:

Heat half of the oil in a large skillet over low heat. Add the onion and garlic; cook, stirring occasionally, until the onion is soft. Increase heat to medium-high, add the chicken, and sauté until chicken is golden brown. Add the chorizo; sauté for 1 minute. Add the rice and stir to coat.

Add the cilantro paste and stock. Stir, then add the clams and mussels. Cover and simmer for 10 minutes or until the clams and mussels start to open. Discard any clams or mussels that do not open. Stir in the kale and season with salt and pepper.

Meanwhile, season the scallops and shrimp with salt and pepper. In a medium skillet, heat the remaining oil over high heat. Sear the scallops until golden brown on each side. Remove from pan. Sauté the shrimp for 2 minutes.

Add the scallops and shrimp to the paella. Garnish with green onions.

STEAMED CARROT CAKE WITH HONEY YOGURT FROSTING

PREP 30 MIN PLUS 6 HOURS FOR DRAINING × COOK 1½ HOURS × SERVES 8

By steaming this cake instead of baking it, you get a ridiculously super-moist dessert. The honey and yogurt frosting is a healthy alternative that gives the traditional carrot cake icing a run for its money.

HONEY YOGURT FROSTING

- 3 cups (750 mL) plain yogurt
- About 3 tablespoons (45 mL) honey
- A pinch of coarse salt
- Zest of 1 lemon

CARROT CAKE

- 1 cup (250 mL) brown sugar
- 1 cup (250 mL) dry bread crumbs
- 1 cup (250 mL) buttermilk
- 3/4 cup (175 mL) molasses
- 1/4 cup (60 mL) canola oil
- 1/4 cup (60 mL) applesauce
- 2 large eggs, beaten
- 1½ cups (375 mL) grated carrots
- 1 cup (250 mL) dried cherries
- 1/2 cup (125 mL) chopped pitted dates
- 2 tablespoons (30 mL) grated fresh ginger
- Zest of 1 orange
- 2 cups (500 mL) all-purpose flour
- 2 teaspoons (10 mL) baking powder
- 1/2 teaspoon (2 mL) baking soda
- 1 teaspoon (5 mL) cinnamon
- 1/2 teaspoon (2 mL) ground ginger
- 1/2 teaspoon (2 mL) ground cloves
- 1/2 teaspoon (2 mL) nutmeg

GARNISH

- Zest of 1 orange

FOR THE FROSTING:

Line a sieve with a double layer of cheesecloth (or a paper coffee filter or paper towel) and set over a bowl. Add the yogurt, cover with plastic wrap, and refrigerate for 6 to 8 hours to drain; the yogurt will have the consistency of soft cream cheese.

In a bowl, whisk together the yogurt, honey to taste, salt, and lemon zest. Refrigerate until needed.

FOR THE CAKE:

Preheat oven to 350°F (180°C). Generously grease an 8-cup (2 L) pudding basin or heatproof bowl.

In a large bowl, combine the brown sugar, bread crumbs, buttermilk, molasses, canola oil, applesauce, eggs, carrots, dried cherries, dates, ginger, and orange zest. In another bowl, sift together the flour, baking powder, baking soda, cinnamon, ginger, cloves, and nutmeg. Add the dry ingredients to the wet ingredients and stir just until combined. Pour the batter into the pudding basin; cover with foil and secure tightly with kitchen string. Place the basin on a rack set in a deep ovenproof pot; add enough hot water to come one-third of the way up the side of the basin. Cover with a lid or foil. Transfer to the oven and steam for 1½ hours or until the cake is set. Remove from the water and let cool on a rack.

To serve, uncover the cake and invert onto a serving dish. Slather the yogurt frosting over the cake. Garnish with grated orange zest right on top.

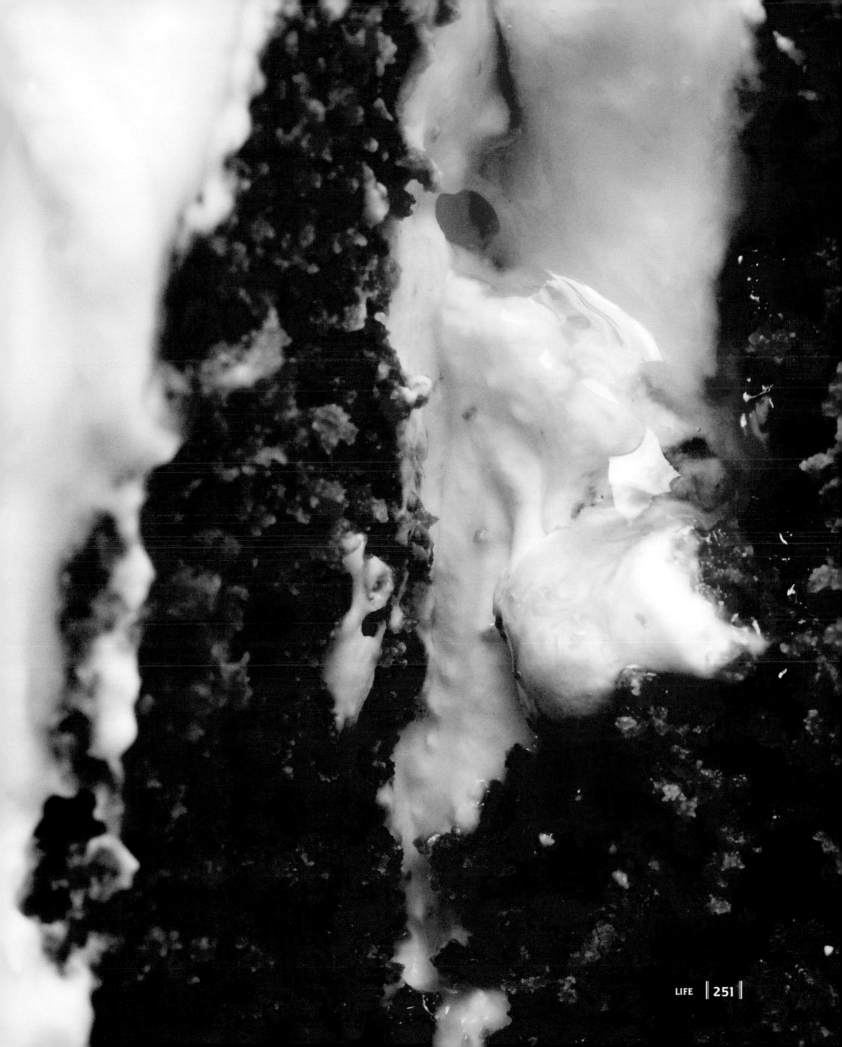

THE
SANDWICH SHOP

KIMCHI
PULLED PORK AND KIMCHI SANDWICH
HOMEMADE BARBECUE CHIPS
CRUDITÉ PLATTER WITH DIPS
COCONUT AND BANANA BREAD PUDDING

Nothing beats the sandwich. All you need is two pieces of bread and the rest is up to you. The possibilities are endless! When you work in a kitchen and you're always on the go, sandwiches are the easiest way to eat. You can have one standing up or walking around, you can save half for later, eat one for breakfast or for a late-night snack—basically any time is a good time to eat a sandwich. In short, they are handheld perfection.

Before we opened Garde Manger, we were there every day doing repairs and renovations. Sometimes my mom would come by and bring us lunch, but most of the time we had to fend for ourselves. We quickly discovered that just around the corner on Rue St-Paul was a great little sandwich shop called Van Winkles, where you can choose from among fresh ingredients and a variety of breads to make your own sandwich. I fell in love not only with Van Winkles's sandwiches (and their giant oatmeal chocolate chip cookies) but also with their owners, a Korean couple, Mr. and Mrs. Lee.

Mrs. Lee makes the sandwiches and Mr. Lee is at the cash, and they're just the nicest, friendliest people. They always greet me with big smiles whenever I walk through the door. They've been in Old Montreal for over twenty-five years, and although their shop isn't fancy, it's a great place. Everything is made to order, and you can see that they put a lot of care into their work. They also have soups, salads, and fresh fruits and vegetables, making it the perfect place to grab a quick bite. All of our staff are addicted to Van Winkles and everyone has their own favourite sandwich. My personal pick used to be turkey and cheese on an onion bun, until . . .

One day I was talking with Mrs. Lee about Korean food, which I had recently become a bit obsessed with. One of my favourite condiments, kimchi, which is made with fermented cabbage, fish sauce, and chilies, was something I wanted to experiment with at the restaurant. Mrs. Lee told me she always made it and had it at the shop, but it was meant for her family and staff—customers never asked for it. She let me taste different batches she had on the go, from the most recent to the oldest. Not everyone likes their kimchi the same, and for me, the more fermented it is, the better. Mrs. Lee couldn't believe I was so into it, but there's something about that spicy, fishy, briny, salty taste that makes me want to put it on everything from hot dogs to crab cakes. Needless to say, my current favourite sandwich at Van Winkles is turkey, cheese, and kimchi on an onion bun.

When I invited Mr. and Mrs. Lee to come to the restaurant, I decided to try to make kimchi just like theirs. Mrs. Lee came right out and told me hers was better, and although we laughed about it, I don't think she was joking. Then they said something to each other in Korean, which I didn't understand, and laughed some more. I got the picture.

I'm happy to announce that Van Winkles has since put kimchi on the menu as a regular sandwich topping, and, as an ode to their meal at my restaurant, they've started doing a pulled pork and kimchi sandwich just like the one I made for them. If you're like me and love kimchi, or you're just curious about this fermented cabbage goodness, I highly suggest you try making it yourself.

KIMCHI

PREP 30 MIN PLUS 4 HOURS FOR BRINING × MAKES 4 CUPS (1 L)

This spicy, briny Korean condiment is going to blow your mind—and your taste buds! Look for Korean red chili powder—called gochugaru—in Asian grocery stores.

BRINED CABBAGE
- 12 cups (3 L) cold water
- 1/4 cup (60 mL) salt
- 1 large napa cabbage, cut in big chunks

KIMCHI
- 1½ cups (375 mL) water
- 1/4 cup (60 mL) rice flour or all-purpose flour
- 2 tablespoons (30 mL) sugar
- 1 onion, chopped
- 3 garlic cloves, minced
- 1-inch (2.5 cm) piece fresh ginger, peeled and coarsely chopped
- 1 lemongrass stalk, minced
- 1/2 cup (125 mL) Korean or other red chili powder
- 2 to 3 large cucumbers, diced
- 5 green onions, minced
- 1/4 cup (60 mL) chopped fresh chives
- 1/4 cup (60 mL) fish sauce

FOR THE BRINED CABBAGE:

In a large nonaluminum bowl or pot, combine the water and salt, stirring to dissolve the salt. Add the cabbage, cover, and refrigerate for 4 hours. Drain the cabbage, rinse thoroughly under cold water, and return to the bowl.

FOR THE KIMCHI:

In a small saucepan, combine the water and rice flour. Bring to a boil over medium-high heat; cook, stirring, for 3 minutes, until thickened. Add the sugar and stir for 1 more minute. Remove from heat and let cool to room temperature.

In a food processor, combine the onion, garlic, ginger, lemongrass, and chili powder; process until smooth. Add the flour mixture; pulse until smooth. Pour over the brined cabbage. Add the cucumbers, green onions, chives, fish sauce, and soy sauce; stir well.

You can enjoy the kimchi fresh right after making it, but I recommend letting it ferment, tightly covered at room temperature, for 24 hours. (*It will keep for 2 weeks, refrigerated.*)

PULLED PORK AND KIMCHI SANDWICH

PREP 45 MIN × COOK 8½ HOURS × SERVES 4

This sandwich, served open-faced and bubbling over with cheese, is pretty much my favourite lunch.

GLAZE

- 1 cup (250 mL) brown sugar
- 1 cup (250 mL) molasses
- 1 cup (250 mL) sweet chili sauce
- 1/2 cup (125 mL) rice wine vinegar
- 1/2 cup (125 mL) soy sauce
- 2 tablespoons (30 mL) minced fresh ginger
- 1 garlic clove, minced
- Salt and freshly cracked black pepper

PULLED PORK

- 1 boneless pork shoulder (5 lb/2.25 kg)
- Whiskey, hickory, or apple wood chips, soaked in water for 1 hour
- Salt and freshly cracked black pepper
- 2 tablespoons (30 mL) canola oil

SANDWICHES

- 4 large submarine buns, split horizontally
- 3 cups (750 mL) shredded mozzarella cheese
- Kimchi (page 256)
- Shredded lettuce

FOR THE GLAZE:

In a medium bowl, combine the brown sugar, molasses, chili sauce, vinegar, soy sauce, ginger, and garlic. Whisk until evenly combined. Season with salt and pepper.

FOR THE PULLED PORK:

Using a smoker, smoke the pork for 2 hours according to manufacturer's directions.

Preheat oven to 300°F (150°C). Season the smoked pork with salt and pepper. Heat the canola oil in a large ovenproof skillet over medium-high heat. Add the pork and sear on all sides.

Pour half of the glaze over the pork. Reserve the rest for adding to the braising liquid later. Cover and transfer to the oven. Cook for 6 hours or until the meat falls off the bone. Let rest in the skillet for 30 minutes.

Transfer the pork to a cutting board. Using a fork, pull the pork meat apart; it will come off in threads. Transfer to a bowl.

Skim the fat from the braising liquid. Add some braising liquid to the shredded meat to moisten it.

Pour the remaining glaze into the skillet with the remaining braising liquid and boil on medium-high heat for 15 minutes or until it thickens. Remove from heat.

FOR THE SANDWICHES:

Arrange the buns cut side up on a baking sheet. Top the buns with pulled pork. Spoon over some of the reduced glaze, and sprinkle with the cheese. Broil until the cheese is melted.

Garnish with kimchi and shredded lettuce.

HOMEMADE BARBECUE CHIPS

PREP 15 MIN × COOK 2 MIN × SERVES 4

I add smoked salt to these crispy homemade potato chips and it makes all the difference.

- 1 teaspoon (5 mL) smoked salt
- 1 teaspoon (5 mL) paprika
- 1 teaspoon (5 mL) chili powder
- 1/2 teaspoon (2 mL) cayenne pepper
- Canola oil for deep-frying
- 4 Yukon Gold potatoes, thinly sliced

In a large bowl, stir together the smoked salt, paprika, chili powder, and cayenne. Set aside.

In a deep-fryer or deep, heavy saucepan, heat 2 inches (5 cm) of canola oil to 350°F (180°C).

Working in batches, fry the potatoes until golden brown and crispy. Drain on paper towels. Toss warm chips with the spices.

CRUDITÉ PLATTER WITH DIPS

PREP 15 MIN × COOK 30 MIN × SERVES 6

Healthy, crunchy, and fresh veggies with dips is one of my favourite after-work snacks.

CARAMELIZED ONION DIP

- 2 tablespoons (30 mL) olive oil
- 1 large onion, thinly sliced
- Coarse salt and freshly cracked black pepper
- 1 cup (250 mL) sour cream
- 1/2 cup (125 mL) cream cheese, softened
- 2 tablespoons (30 mL) smoked paprika

ROASTED GARLIC AÏOLI

- 1 large head of roasted garlic (page 150)
- 1 garlic clove, minced
- 2 large egg yolks
- Juice of 1 lemon
- 2 tablespoons (30 mL) water
- 1/2 teaspoon (2 mL) cayenne pepper
- Salt and freshly cracked black pepper
- 1 cup (250 mL) olive oil

WARM BUTTERED HUMMUS

- 2 cups (500 mL) dried chickpeas, soaked in water overnight
- 1 garlic clove, minced
- Zest and juice of 1 lemon
- 1/2 cup (125 mL) butter
- 1/2 cup (125 mL) extra-virgin olive oil
- 1 teaspoon (5 mL) ground cumin
- Salt and freshly cracked black pepper
- 3 tablespoons (45 mL) butter, melted and still warm
- 1 Roma tomato, chopped
- 1/2 cup (125 mL) pitted kalamata olives, chopped
- 2 green onions, chopped

FOR SERVING

- Warm pita breads
- Sugar snap peas, blanched
- Baby carrots with stems
- Celery ribs
- Radishes
- Cauliflower florets, blanched
- Broccoli florets, blanched
- Endives

FOR THE CARAMELIZED ONION DIP:

Heat the oil in a large skillet over medium-low heat. Add the onions and cook, stirring occasionally, until caramelized, about 30 minutes. Season with salt and black pepper. Let cool. In a medium bowl, combine the sour cream, cream cheese, paprika, and onions; stir until well combined.

FOR THE ROASTED GARLIC AÏOLI:

In a blender, combine the roasted garlic, minced garlic, egg yolks, lemon juice, water, cayenne, and salt and black pepper to taste. Blend until smooth. With the motor running, slowly add the olive oil, blending until emulsified. Add a little more water if needed to thin the consistency.

FOR THE WARM BUTTERED HUMMUS:

In a large saucepan, combine the drained chickpeas with 8 cups (2 L) of water. Simmer until very tender, at least 25 minutes. Drain the chickpeas, reserving a few tablespoons of water. In a food processor, combine the hot chickpeas, garlic, lemon zest and juice, 1/2 cup (125 mL) butter, olive oil, and cumin. Process until smooth. Season with salt and pepper.

Transfer to a serving bowl and drizzle with warm melted butter. Top with chopped tomato, olives, and green onions.

COCONUT AND BANANA BREAD PUDDING

PREP 25 MIN PLUS 1 HOUR FOR SOAKING × COOK 50 MIN × SERVES 8

Coconut, bananas, and chocolate. I don't think I need to say anything more.

COCONUT AND BANANA BREAD PUDDING

- 4 large eggs
- 1 cup (250 mL) coconut milk
- 1 cup (250 mL) whole milk
- 1/4 cup (60 mL) brown sugar
- 2 teaspoons (10 mL) grated fresh ginger
- 2 teaspoons (10 mL) vanilla extract
- A pinch of salt
- 1 loaf brioche, cubed (about 6 cups/1.5 L)
- 1 ripe banana, diced
- 1/2 cup (125 mL) chopped bittersweet chocolate (3 oz/85 g)
- 1/4 cup (60 mL) shredded coconut

BUTTER RUM SAUCE

- 1/4 cup (60 mL) butter
- 1/2 cup (125 mL) brown sugar
- 1/4 cup (60 mL) whipping cream
- 2 tablespoons (30 mL) rum (optional)
- A pinch of salt

GARNISHES

- Whipped cream
- Toasted coconut shavings

FOR THE BREAD PUDDING:

In a bowl, whisk together the eggs, coconut milk, whole milk, brown sugar, ginger, vanilla, and salt. Add the bread and stir so it absorbs the mixture. Stir in the banana and chocolate. Refrigerate for 1 hour before baking.

Preheat oven to 350°F (180°C). Butter eight 6-oz (175 mL) ramekins and arrange ramekins on a baking sheet. Divide the batter among the ramekins. Sprinkle with shredded coconut. Bake for 50 minutes or until the pudding is puffed and golden.

FOR THE BUTTER RUM SAUCE:

In a small saucepan, melt the butter over medium heat. Add the brown sugar, cream, rum (if using), and salt; whisk until well combined. Simmer, whisking frequently, until thickened, about 5 minutes. Remove from heat.

Serve the puddings warm with the butter rum sauce, whipped cream, and toasted coconut shavings.

Shallots
store cheesecloth paper
1x 10 day soak
9x rock shrimps
3x crabs shell
TO KNMH

2 x Shrimp.
2 x Crab
BUY SEAWEED!
MARION 32
VALEVILLE 38
CHIASSON 60
lucky 19

lobster
w/ crab

tows
chicken bone
veal bones
chicken legs
Filet

dirty
x 1yr cheddar

REGULARS

PRESERVED LEMONS
SMOKED BARBECUED PORK WITH WATERCRESS SALAD
ROASTED FILLET OF GROUPER WITH PAN-ROASTED CIPOLLINI AND TOMATOES
SAUTÉED KALE WITH MORELS
POUDING CHÔMEUR

If there's one thing a restaurant cannot survive without, it's regulars. They really are the backbone of the business. They're a big part of who we are, and we wouldn't be here today without their constant support of Garde Manger. It's great to have the same people come in week after week, because although they started off as familiar faces, they've ended up as family.

It feels so good to know that there are people out there who have fully embraced our approach to food and dining. They've become part of our success and have been through all the ups and downs with us. They've seen staff come and go, watched the menu evolve, they've eaten in the restaurant when it was practically empty in the dead of winter and have barely gotten in the door on busy nights in the summer. While not every experience they've had was seamless, it's a huge sign of respect that after seven years in the business, our regulars still keep coming back. We must be doing something right! It's a tremendously rewarding feeling, and at the end of the day, it validates all of our hard work.

Don't get me wrong—we treat everyone the same, whether it's your first time or your fiftieth, whether you're from Tennessee or right around the corner. But there's something about the longevity of a regular. When I look around the dining room today and still see some of those friendly faces that came to eat when we first opened our doors, I know we're on the right track.

You'd be surprised how much the regulars influence our dishes and what goes on the menu. Our regulars are, well, regulars, so they're here a lot and have a pretty good idea of what works and what doesn't. We expect them to be honest with us, offer constructive criticism on how things can be improved, and

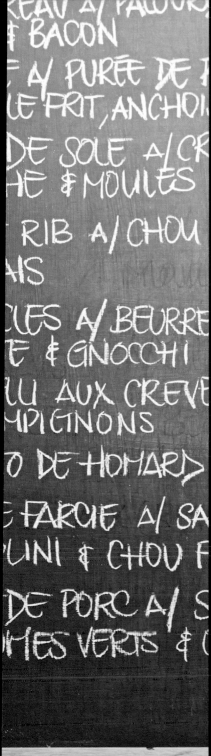

we always listen to them because their feedback is of the utmost importance to us.

More than just customers, regulars are engaged in all our lives. They want to know how my hockey game went on the weekend, if my dog is feeling better, if we found a new bartender. They've become part of our restaurant family, and I hope they feel the same about us.

Max, Dominique, Dr. Dolman and his wife, Colette, Gassia, Jeff, Mark, Kelly, and all the other regulars past and present—thank you for all of your consistent support and for making our jobs worth doing.

PRESERVED LEMONS

PREP 10 MIN PLUS 1 WEEK FOR CURING × MAKES 8 LEMONS

Less tart than fresh lemons, this staple of Moroccan cuisine keeps forever—and it looks nice in a Mason jar on the countertop too.

- 8 lemons
- 2 cups (500 mL) coarse salt
- 1½ cups (375 mL) lemon juice
- 1 tablespoon (15 mL) black peppercorns
- 4 kaffir lime leaves

Wash the lemons very well and pat dry. Cut each lemon into 4 wedges, cutting to within 1/2 inch (1 cm) of the bottom to keep the lemons whole. Remove all the seeds.

Place the lemons in a sterilized large jar. Add the salt, lemon juice, peppercorns, and lime leaves; put on the lid and shake well. Add more lemon juice if necessary to just cover the lemons. Seal and refrigerate. Shake the jar every day or two to help dissolve the salt. Allow the lemons to cure for at least 1 week. Rinse under cold water before using.

SMOKED BARBECUED PORK WITH WATERCRESS SALAD

PREP 30 MIN PLUS 12 HOURS FOR MARINATING × COOK 30 MIN × SERVES 4 TO 6

Cheap and easy, this pork loin with an Asian barbecue seasoning makes a great summer meal.

PORK

- 1/2 cup (125 mL) soy sauce
- 1/2 cup (125 mL) orange juice
- 2 tablespoons (30 mL) grated fresh ginger
- 1 garlic clove, minced
- 2 pork tenderloins
- Freshly cracked black pepper
- 2 handfuls of hickory wood chips, soaked in water for 1 hour
- 1 cup (250 mL) water
- 1 cup (250 mL) ice cubes

WATERCRESS SALAD

- A bunch of watercress, tough stems discarded
- 1 shallot, thinly sliced
- 4 hard-boiled eggs, chopped
- Maldon sea salt and freshly cracked black pepper

CREAMY HONEY DIJON DRESSING

- 2 tablespoons (30 mL) mayonnaise
- 1 tablespoon (15 mL) Dijon mustard
- 1 teaspoon (5 mL) honey
- Juice of 1/2 lemon
- Salt and freshly cracked black pepper

TO MARINATE THE PORK:
In a large bowl, combine the soy sauce, orange juice, ginger, and garlic. Add the pork, turning to coat. Cover and refrigerate for at least 12 hours.

TO SMOKE THE PORK:
Remove the pork from the marinade, discarding the marinade. Pat dry with paper towels. Put the pork on a plate and refrigerate for 1 hour to dry out.

Prepare a wok smoker: Line a large bamboo steamer with parchment paper. Lay two sheets of foil in the bottom of a wok. Place drained wood chips on top. Turn heat to high. Add water. Lay the pork in the bamboo steamer; season with pepper. Place ice cubes in a heatproof measuring cup in the steamer next to the pork to create a cold smoke. Set the steamer inside the smoking wok. Cover and smoke, keeping the temperature under 150°F (65°C), for 20 minutes.

Preheat grill to high. Grill the pork for about 5 minutes on each side. (Pork may also be cooked in a large skillet until browned but still slightly pink inside.)

FOR THE WATERCRESS SALAD:
In a bowl, toss the watercress with the shallot and eggs. Season with Maldon salt and pepper.

FOR THE CREAMY HONEY DIJON DRESSING:
In a small bowl, combine the mayonnaise, mustard, honey, and lemon juice; whisk well. Season with salt and pepper.

To serve, toss the salad with the dressing. Slice the pork and arrange on plates or a platter. Top with the watercress salad.

ROASTED FILLET OF GROUPER WITH PAN-ROASTED CIPOLLINI AND TOMATOES

PREP 20 MIN PLUS 1 HOUR FOR MARINATING × COOK 1 HOUR × SERVES 8 TO 10

The sweetness of the onion and tomato combination, along with a fresh herb salad on top, makes this fish dinner a cut above.

GARLIC CONFIT
- 1 cup (250 mL) olive oil
- 12 garlic cloves, peeled

GROUPER
- 3 tablespoons (45 mL) olive oil
- Leaves from 4 sprigs of rosemary, minced
- Leaves from 4 sprigs of thyme, minced
- 1 fresh red chili, finely chopped
- 1 fresh skin-on grouper fillet (2 lb/900 g)
- Salt and freshly cracked black pepper

PAN-ROASTED CIPOLLINI AND TOMATOES
- 1 tablespoon (15 mL) olive oil
- About 12 cipollini onions, peeled
- About 24 cherry tomatoes
- 2 tablespoons (30 mL) butter
- Salt and freshly cracked black pepper

FOR SERVING
- 3 tablespoons (45 mL) finely chopped preserved lemon (page 270)
- A drizzle of extra-virgin olive oil
- A handful of fresh cilantro leaves
- A handful of chopped fresh parsley
- Maldon sea salt and freshly cracked black pepper

FOR THE GARLIC CONFIT:
Heat the oil and garlic in a small saucepan over low heat until the garlic is tender, about 30 minutes. Strain, reserving the flavoured oil for another use. Set aside the garlic confit.

FOR THE GROUPER:
Using a mortar and pestle, mash half of the olive oil, half of the garlic confit, rosemary, thyme, and chili into a paste. Rub the paste over the fish; cover with plastic wrap and refrigerate for 1 hour.

Preheat oven to 350°F (180°C).

Heat the remaining olive oil in a large ovenproof skillet over medium-high heat. Season the fish with salt and pepper. Sear on the skin side until crisp and golden brown, about 5 minutes. Transfer to the oven and continue cooking until the flesh is flaky, about 25 minutes.

FOR THE PAN-ROASTED CIPOLLINI AND TOMATOES:
While the fish is roasting, in another large skillet, heat the oil over medium-high heat. Add the cipollini; sauté until tender, about 10 minutes. Increase heat to high. Add the tomatoes and the remaining garlic confit; sauté until the cipollini are golden brown, about 5 minutes. Swirl in the butter and season with salt and pepper.

To serve, transfer the grouper to a platter. Top with preserved lemon and drizzle with olive oil. Spoon the roasted cipollini and tomatoes over the fish. Garnish with cilantro and parsley. Sprinkle with Maldon salt and pepper.

SAUTÉED KALE WITH MORELS

PREP 15 MIN PLUS 30 MIN FOR SOAKING × COOK 25 MIN × SERVES 4

In this recipe, I cook mushrooms in veal stock so that when you throw in the blanched kale near the end, it soaks up all the delicious cooking juices.

- 4 oz (115 g) dried morels
- 2 tablespoons (30 mL) butter
- 1 tablespoon (15 mL) olive oil
- 1 shallot, minced
- 1 garlic clove, minced
- Maldon sea salt and freshly cracked black pepper
- Leaves from 2 sprigs of thyme, finely chopped
- 2 tablespoons (30 mL) balsamic vinegar
- 1 cup (250 mL) veal stock
- 1 lb (450 g) kale, stems and thick centre ribs discarded, leaves blanched and chopped

Soak morels in hot water until softened, about 30 minutes. Strain morels in a fine-mesh sieve, reserving the soaking liquid. Rinse the morels well and pat dry.

Heat the butter and oil in a large skillet over medium-high heat until the butter is melted. Add the shallot and garlic; sauté for 5 minutes or until the shallot is translucent. Add the morels; season with salt and pepper. Add the thyme; continue cooking for another 5 minutes. Stir in the balsamic vinegar and let evaporate. Add the veal stock and morel soaking liquid; cook until the stock is reduced by half, about 10 minutes.

Stir in the kale; continue cooking for 2 minutes. Remove from heat and season with Maldon salt and pepper.

POUDING CHÔMEUR

PREP 15 MIN × COOK 40 MIN × SERVES 8

Also known as Poor Man's Pudding, this Québécois dessert was created during the Depression by female factory workers. Using cheap ingredients like flour, water, and sugar, it was easy to make and didn't require hard-to-find eggs. My version is just as easy, and I've added maple syrup for a true regional treat.

MAPLE SAUCE

- **2 cups (500 mL) maple syrup**
- **1 cup (250 mL) whipping cream**
- **1/2 cup (125 mL) brown sugar**
- **1/4 cup (60 mL) butter**

BATTER

- **1 cup (250 mL) butter, softened**
- **1 cup (250 mL) sugar**
- **1 tablespoon (15 mL) vanilla extract**
- **2 cups (500 mL) all-purpose flour**
- **2 teaspoons (10 mL) baking powder**
- **A pinch of salt**
- **1 cup (250 mL) milk**

FOR SERVING

- **Vanilla ice cream**

FOR THE MAPLE SAUCE:
In a medium saucepan, combine the maple syrup, cream, brown sugar, and butter. Bring to a boil, reduce heat, and simmer for 5 minutes. Remove from heat.

FOR THE BATTER:
Preheat oven to 350°F (180°C). Arrange eight 6-oz (175 mL) ramekins on a baking sheet.

In a large bowl, cream the butter with the sugar and vanilla. In another bowl, whisk together the flour, baking powder, and salt. Add the flour mixture to the butter mixture, alternating with the milk, making 3 additions of the flour mixture and 2 of milk, and beating after each addition until just combined.

Divide the batter among the ramekins. Pour the maple sauce over the batter. Bake for 35 minutes or until golden brown and a toothpick inserted into the centre of the pudding comes out clean.

Serve warm with a scoop of vanilla ice cream.

ACKNOWLEDGMENTS

To everyone who helped make *Chuck's Day Off*, the TV show or the book, happen—from the production team to the restaurant staff, to the suppliers, to the "eaters," to the network, to the bands, thanks.

Jessica Midlash, Dermai Young, Shannon McGarr, David Rozon, Zoe Marshall Nares, Theo Lerikos, Alan Ricardo Aguirre Ramos, Malcolm J. Travis, Antoni Porowski, Ferelith Young, Fabien Welp-Barr, Gianpaolo Venuta, Marieve Kochenberger, Shawn Glasgow, Chantal Godbout, Chris Lacy, Genevieve Van Gyte, Olivier Bastien, Lisa-Marie Leblanc, Carolina Bartzak, John Liboiron, Jean-François Méthot, Sarah Hamlin, Colin Trudel, Julie Marquis, Nicholas Zypchen, Vanessa Trahan, Genevieve Pelletier, Steve Kellison, Bryce Kaufman, Rolando Zuniga, Ian Nelson, Christina Nordquist, Jason Joseph, Mitul Patel, Marc Filzer, Eugene Carpine, Vilashi Patel, Jamie Wilson, Theodore Garner-Meltzer, Marieve Hamel, Erik Frank, Skyler Blue, Raffi Melnick-Beinglas, Brooke Beaudin, Andrew Maibroda, Alex Thiffault, Niki Pislis, Olivia Nowak, Catherine Ouellette, Celeste Ross Opazo, Nhu Ahn Phan, Thomas Carney, Annie-Claude Roy, Diemu Kalunda, Jason Voltaire, Trevor Wheatley, Quinn Downes, Katerine Marois, Isabelle Abergel, Patrik Balek, Max Ruiz Laing, Genevieve Bertrand, Jonathan Thomas, Eve Legault, Todd Bolton, Andrew Davidson, Florence Ross Opazo, Maxime Ouimet, Morgan Mallory, Matthieu Gagnon, Vincent Carney, Kevin Tolton, Hart Goetze, Alexia Baillargon, Tim Robertson, Rebecca Jane Wilson, Webster Galman, Brendan White, Maude Trepanier, Curtis Collier, Dave Gill, Camille Reed Brissonet, Farida Khan, Pierre-Olivier Besner, Ryan D'Amico, Nazli Var, Matthew Graham, Xavier Rousseau, Michael Bukacheski, Sarah Laporta, Amanda Bullock, Cedric Bezanson, Paul Anderson, Emanuel Tremblay, Thomas Prince, Michele Tili, Luke Anderson, Sabrina Cussen, Ilyaa Ghafouri, Jane Ross Opazo, Kathleen Cunningham, Marco Degregorio, Keero Birla, Catherine Pilon, Debbie Travis, Hans Rosenstein, Scott Bailey, Anne-Marie Withenshaw, Johanne Depelteau, Patti Murphy, Eric St-Hilaire, Barry Russell, Patrick Villeneuve, Patrick Villeneuve, Marie-Laure Sénéchal, Amanda Matalanis, Roxanna Macedo, Jean-Philippe Audet, David Shohet, Nicolas Petsilas, Francois Blanchette, Murray Nicol, Louis-Vincent Blaquière, Michel, Auclair, Yannick Castonguay, Donat Chabot, Stephan Peterson, Yannick Di Vito, Stephan Menghi, Joanna Fox, Erin Reich, Lisa Leblanc, Isabel Leblanc, Isabel Ramirez, Emily Leonard, Robb Jamieson, Emilia Kate Jamieson, Daniel Haber, Chris Agoston, Anne Côté, Paola Ridolfi, Michel Caron, Jonathan Wenk, Adam Frappier, Ken Coolen, Karine Atalla, Jilian Spingel, Kalvin Kimball, Lynne Trepanier, Eric Roy, Jean Asselin, Stéphane Kirouac, Hugo Roy, Justin Lamarche, Olivier Labonté-Lemoyne, Mathieu Poirier, Simon Lamarre, Yannick Morisset, Olivier Poisson, Jean-François Bertrand, Mathieu Beauchamps, Francis Fortin, Jonathan Tremblay, Philippe Boily, Max Rosenstein, Wayne Busby, Simon Theriault, Sonya Holmes, José Poulain, Rehka Birla, Ian MacMillan, Devon Ravary, Jenny Langton, Daniel Beirne, Susannah Heath-Eves, Andrew Labelle, Thomas Harper, Kale Reum, Marie-Alexandra Forget, Lesley Jacobi, Greg Thompson, Julian Morelli, J. Enrique H. Careaga, Andrew Kemp, Akritas Akritopoulos, Martin Nault, Stephane Dietiker, Cristina Cugliandro, Nikola Markovic, Leah Michaud, Melissa De Masi, Thomas Ouellet, Lyndsey O'Keefe, Brenda Newman, Rebecca Arsenault, Angela DePalma, Paul Pivetta, Dominic Barbe, Studio Harmonie, Annie Kaprielian, Pota Manolakos, David Kaprielian, Katy Corriveau, Sue Wheeler, Maresa McLaren, Talia Aznavour, Emily Cholette, Kate Saint George, Leslie Merklinger, Emily Morgan, Brynn Tschirhart, Cathy Kurzbock, Jaclyn Atwood, Christine Geddes, John Withenshaw, Jay Walker, Stephanie Keating, Jen Jones, Dominique Lafond, Marc-Andre Lavoie, Kirsten Hanson, Greg Tabor, Noelle Zitzer, Shaun Oakey, Neil Erickson, Leo MacDonald, Maylene Loveland, James Baran, Kyle Marshall, Tim Rozon, Costa & Sam, Eli & Barbara Kurtzman, Mazen, Roberto & Bokhai, Alex, Peter, David & Howard, Robert Pendergast, Norm Weekes, Isabelle Basuk, Brittany Weekes & Taelyr Weekes, David McMillan & Fred Morin, Yan Paquette & Richard Dan, Thibault Galissaire, Safwan, Carmella, Jordi & Yakari, Charles & The Bierbrier Crew, Theo Diamantis, Marie France Levesque & Romy Dupal-Demers, Stephen Mcleod & Tye Hunt, Maxime, Yannick & Jonathan, Paolo Scala, Yves Baudry, André Querion & Pierrot Fortier, Melissa De Forte, Jasmine Patry, Lotus Ellis, Kate Ellis & JR Ellis, John Ruffner, Ken Eekhof, Erin Reich, Raphael Melnick-Banglas, Mireille Olano Kostopoulos, Pat Dumont, Daniel Mireault, Eddy Amoroso, Jeanne Lefebvre, Theo Gardner, Mohammed Deramchi, Catherine Brossard, Fred Laurent, Eugenio Carpine, Mohamed, Benoit Godin, Erica Dancose, Amedee Lavallée, Complexe Hockey Bonaventure, Carl Adam, Harold Scharf, Derek Curtis, Tom Peacode, Louis Mazerolle, Steven Wheeler, Johanna Donovan, Nick Gallagher, Michael Stearns, Paul St Pierre

Plamondon, Alexia Jensen, Pascal Fortin, Mark Bandrayk, William Hilbchuk, H. Libchae, C. Deruchie, Ron Nielsen, Nick Scheib, Marc Dunn, C. Matossian, Will Cundill, Avi Steinberg, Tania Tassone, Peter J. Cullen, John Fairbrother, Lucia Cimaglia, Hivron Turanli, Paolo Macchi, Costa Tsoudis, Helen Papadatos, George Tsoudis, Maria Vlahos, Yong Koo Lee, Insuk Lee, Eve Werbrouck, Olivier Caron, Maryse Fournier, Christina, Cathy Krcezinac, Jessica Carter, Antoinette Dejong, Francine Hébert, Pierre Hébert, Ben Hébert, Phil Hébert, Aunt Danie, Uncle George, Sabrina, Dan Hébert, Nancy Hébert, Brent Hébert, Charlie Hébert, Claude Bélanger, Hélene Bélanger, Lea Bélanger, Laurent Bélanger, Mamie, Chuck Hughes II, Nicholas Zypcher, Sam Barr, Diana Levine, Howard Abboud, Kimberly Janas, Myriam Achard, Victoria Dumont, Carl Adjami, Claudio, Nico, Daniel Glick, Nick Farkas, Evenko, Brigitte Maillette, Michel Guérin, Noémie Guérin-Maillette, Les Fromages du Verger, Marika Moshonas, France Leclerc, Effie Lordanidis, Tony Moshonas, MONAS & CO LTD, Manon Chaput, Gilles Jourdendis, La Fromagerie Atwater, Dr. William Fisher, Wedlyne Pierre, Pierre-Marc Poirier, Alain Salinovich, David Angus, Rachel Hawes, Rebecca Burns, Edbert C. Abad, Edgardo Abad, Kriselda, M.O.M, Marie-Fleur St-Pierre, Tracy Winkworth, Emma Cardarelli, Dominique Shoofey, Dr. Barry Dolman, Colette Dolman, Gassia Kazandjian, Jeffrey Buran, Mark London, Kelly, Ryan Gray, John Bills, Daniel Notkin, Chris Heppner, Dave Rozon, PECNORD, Vanya Filipovic, Jon Webb, Lucky Luc Calèche, Martine Bourassa, Kevin Rochford, Guillaume Lafrance, Kevin Rochford, Larry Wanagas, Serge Sargento, Pascal Roberge, Diane Lametti, Frank McDonough, Kieran Roy, Marcello Favia, Dave Guenette, Jonathan Simkin, Jennifer Meyer, Neil Harris, Caitlin Veitch, Dane Deviller, Sean Hosein, Dave Gen, Francoise de Grandpre, Justin Bumper Reeve, Gino Olivieri, Geneviève Côté, Philippe-Aubert Messier, Louis-Philippe Caron, Avi Diamond, Franz Schuller, Jennifer Mitchell, Trevor Larocque, Eoin O Leary, Ryan Spalding, Caitlin Veitch, Joe Ferland, Beast, The Trews, Two Hours Traffic, Arkells, Bedouin Soundclash, Dee, Creature, Mobile, Sam Roberts, Zeus, Jason Collett, Hollerado, The Stills, Apostle of Hustle, Yukon Blonde, Daniel Wesley, Dragonette, Hawksley Workman, Hedley, Jason Bajada, K-os, Mistress Barbara, We Are Wolves, The Junction, Vulgaires Machins, Colin Moore, Misteur Valaire, You Say Party, Winter Gloves, Stars, Attack in Black, The Zolas.

INDEX